CRITICAL CHOICES

Navigating High-Stakes Business Scenarios

CONSULTORIA IA

Copyright © 2024 CONSULTORIA IA

All rights reserved

The characters and events portrayed in this book are fictitious. Any similarity to real persons, living or dead, is coincidental and not intended by the author.

No part of this book may be reproduced, or stored in a retrieval system, or transmitted in any form or by any means, electronic, mechanical, photocopying, recording, or otherwise, without express written permission of the publisher.

Cover design by: Art Painter
Library of Congress Control Number: 2018675309
Printed in the United States of America

TO OUR FAMILY

CONTENTS

Title Page

Copyright

Dedication

Brief synopsis

Target Audience

Why Read This Book?

Preface

Chapter 1: The Pressure Cooker: Making Decisions Under Uncertainty

Chapter 2: Strategic Pivot Points: When to Change Course and Why

Chapter 3: Leading Through Crisis: Turning Challenges into Opportunities

Chapter 4: Navigating Conflict: Managing Stakeholders and Competing Interests

Step 1: Crafting a Clear, Compelling Vision for Global Expansion

Step 2: Understanding and Addressing Stakeholder Motivations

Step 3: Transparent and Regular Communication

Step 4: Aligning Incentives and Building a Sense of Ownership

Chapter 5: The Long Game: Balancing Short-Term Gains with Long-Term Vision

Appendices

BRIEF SYNOPSIS

In **"Critical Choices: Navigating High-Stakes Business Scenarios"**, decision-makers are equipped with the tools and frameworks to excel under pressure. This book delves into real-world examples of high-stakes business situations where every choice can determine success or failure. From managing crises and mergers to navigating competitive landscapes, it explores how leaders can sharpen their decision-making processes, minimize risks, and strategically assess outcomes. Packed with actionable insights, this guide empowers executives to make informed, decisive moves that drive long-term success in today's volatile business environment.

TARGET AUDIENCE

The target audience for Critical Choices: Navigating High-Stakes Business Scenarios includes:

- C-suite Executives: CEOs, CFOs, COOs, and other top-level leaders who make critical decisions that impact the direction and success of their organizations.

- Entrepreneurs and Business Owners: Those running their own businesses and facing high-pressure decisions in a competitive market.

- Strategic Planners and Decision Makers: Individuals involved in long-term planning and risk management within their companies.

- Business Consultants and Advisors: Professionals who guide companies through complex and high-stakes scenarios.

- MBA Students and Business Scholars: Future business leaders seeking practical insights into navigating critical business decisions.

This book is ideal for those who thrive in or are preparing for environments where high-stakes decisions define success or failure.

WHY READ THIS BOOK?

Critical Choices: Navigating High-Stakes Business Scenarios offers essential insights for anyone in leadership or aspiring to make impactful decisions in today's fast-paced business world. Here's why it stands out:

1. Real-World Case Studies: The book is packed with real-world examples of companies that thrived or failed based on pivotal decisions, providing valuable lessons for navigating similar situations.

2. Strategic Decision-Making Frameworks: Learn practical frameworks to assess risks, weigh options, and make decisions under pressure, ensuring that you can tackle high-stakes challenges with confidence.

3. Expert Insights: Get access to expert opinions and strategies from seasoned business leaders and decision-makers who've been in the trenches.

4. Proven Tactics for High-Stress Scenarios: Whether you're dealing with a crisis, launching a new initiative, or facing market disruptions, this book provides proven tactics for making sound decisions in high-pressure situations.

5. Adaptability in Uncertainty: In an era of rapid change and uncertainty, this book equips you with the tools to stay adaptable, proactive, and resilient, ensuring long-term success in an unpredictable environment.

PREFACE

In business, there are moments when decisions feel like they carry the weight of the world. A single choice can shape the future of an organization, determine its trajectory, and impact the lives of countless people. These are the critical choices—the moments of high stakes where failure is not an option, and the consequences of hesitation or miscalculation can be devastating.

As entrepreneurs, executives, and business leaders, we know these moments well. We've all faced the pressure of choosing between equally uncertain paths, of balancing innovation with risk, of responding to crises with limited information, and of managing teams when everything is on the line. These moments define our careers, our companies, and even our industries.

This book was born from our collective experiences of navigating such high-stakes business scenarios. Drawing from real-life examples, case studies, and proven decision-making frameworks, Critical Choices: Navigating High-Stakes Business Scenarios is designed to be a guide for anyone facing pivotal moments in their professional journey. Whether you are an experienced CEO, a startup founder, or a business strategist, this book provides you with practical tools and insights to make smarter, more confident decisions when the pressure is on.

Our aim is simple: to empower you to navigate uncertainty with clarity, confidence, and resilience. Through the pages of this book, we hope to offer you not only strategic frameworks but also the mindset needed to thrive in today's complex business landscape. In an era defined by rapid change and constant disruption, the ability to make critical decisions quickly and effectively is no longer just a skill—it's a necessity.

As you read, we encourage you to reflect on your own business challenges and decisions. Think of this book as a resource you can return to whenever you're at a crossroads. In those moments of high stakes, we hope these insights will help guide you toward the right choice for you, your team, and your organization.

Welcome to Critical Choices. The stakes are high, but so are the rewards.

Sincerely,

CONSULTORIA IA

2024

CHAPTER 1: THE PRESSURE COOKER: MAKING DECISIONS UNDER UNCERTAINTY

Understanding the Stakes

Making decisions under uncertainty is an inevitable aspect of modern business leadership. In today's hyper-competitive and fast-paced market, leaders are constantly faced with ambiguity, where decisions need to be made quickly and with incomplete information. Whether it's navigating a financial crisis, responding to sudden shifts in consumer behavior, or addressing unexpected disruptions such as supply chain breakdowns or technological failures, the stakes are always high. Leaders are often confronted with pressure cooker environments, where every choice can have far-reaching consequences not just for the organization but also for its stakeholders, employees, and customers.

Understanding the stakes of decision-making in such environments is crucial because these choices often define the trajectory of businesses. A well-calculated move can lead to a competitive advantage, securing market share and long-term growth, while a poorly considered decision could result in significant losses, damage to reputation, or even organizational collapse. Thus, the ability to navigate high-stakes scenarios with confidence and clarity separates effective leaders from the rest. But how can leaders develop the skills necessary to thrive under pressure? It begins with acknowledging the weight of uncertainty and learning to manage it systematically.

The key challenge here is not the uncertainty itself but the paralysis it can induce. In high-stakes situations, leaders must resist the temptation to overanalyze or delay action in the hope that perfect information will materialize. In reality, waiting too long for clarity can be just as damaging as making the wrong move. Therefore, mastering the art of decision-making in uncertain conditions is about balancing speed with accuracy, intuition with analysis, and immediate needs with long-term goals. This chapter will explore the strategies and mindsets that allow leaders to thrive under such intense conditions, offering practical tools to help them navigate these "pressure cooker" moments with resilience and confidence.

Navigating the Fear of Failure

One of the greatest psychological barriers to decision-making under uncertainty is the fear of failure. When the stakes are high, the fear of making the wrong choice can paralyze even the most experienced leaders. This fear is not unfounded; every decision comes with inherent risks, and in high-pressure scenarios, the margin for error is often slim. However, while failure is a possibility, it should not deter action. Successful leaders understand that failure is not the end but part of the learning process. They embrace the possibility of mistakes as an opportunity to gain insights and refine their approach.

To overcome the fear of failure, leaders must develop a mindset that views challenges as opportunities rather than threats. This requires a shift from a fixed to a growth-oriented perspective, where failure is seen as a stepping stone toward improvement. Cultivating this mindset involves embracing resilience and adaptability, learning to pivot quickly when things don't go as planned, and maintaining a focus on long-term goals despite short-term setbacks.

The fear of failure can be mitigated by fostering a culture of psychological safety within the organization. When employees feel safe to express concerns, challenge assumptions, and offer alternative perspectives without fear of retribution, it encourages more robust decision-making. Leaders who promote open communication and collaboration are better equipped to gather diverse insights and make informed choices, even in uncertain environments.

Leveraging Data, But Not Relying Solely on It

In today's data-driven world, leaders often turn to analytics and metrics to guide their decisions. Data can provide valuable insights into trends, patterns, and potential outcomes, making it a powerful tool in uncertain scenarios. However, while data is an important asset, it should not be the sole determinant of decision-making, especially in high-stakes situations where time is of the essence and comprehensive data may be unavailable.

Leaders must learn to balance data with intuition and experience. In a "pressure cooker" environment, there may not be enough time to gather or analyze all the necessary data. Waiting for more information can lead to missed opportunities or exacerbate a crisis. Instead, leaders should use the data they have as one piece of a broader decision-making framework, incorporating their intuition, experience, and knowledge of the business landscape to fill in the gaps. This ability to make quick, informed decisions without complete data is a hallmark of effective leadership.

Additionally, data itself can be misleading if not properly interpreted. In uncertain situations, it's easy to become overwhelmed by the sheer volume of available information, leading to analysis paralysis. Leaders must develop the skill of discerning which data points are most relevant to the decision at hand and avoid getting bogged down in irrelevant details. This requires a clear understanding of the business's goals, the specific challenges it faces, and the broader market context in which it operates.

The Role of Emotional Intelligence

Emotional intelligence (EI) plays a critical role in decision-making under uncertainty. Leaders with high emotional intelligence are better equipped to handle the pressure, stress, and ambiguity that come with high-stakes decisions. They are able to remain calm under pressure, manage their emotions, and maintain focus on the task at hand, which is essential when making critical decisions that impact the future of the organization.

Emotional intelligence helps leaders understand the emotions of others and navigate interpersonal dynamics during stressful situations. When uncertainty looms, teams often look to their leaders for guidance and reassurance. Leaders who can demonstrate empathy, communicate effectively, and inspire confidence can foster a sense of unity and purpose, even in challenging times. This emotional support can be the difference between a team that crumbles under pressure and one that rises to the occasion.

Leaders can cultivate emotional intelligence by practicing self-awareness, regulating their emotions, and developing empathy. By staying attuned to their own emotional responses and those of their team, they can create a supportive environment that encourages clear thinking and decisive action. Emotional intelligence also enhances a leader's ability to manage conflict, which is often inevitable in high-pressure situations where differing opinions and stress levels can lead to tension.

Scenario Planning and Contingency Strategies

One of the most effective ways to prepare for high-stakes decisions is through scenario planning. This involves anticipating potential future events, identifying key uncertainties, and developing strategies for various possible outcomes. By thinking through different scenarios in advance, leaders can reduce the element of surprise and make more informed decisions when uncertainty arises.

Scenario planning encourages leaders to consider a wide range of possibilities, from best-case to worst-case scenarios. It also helps them identify the critical variables that could impact their decision-making and prepare contingency plans to address those variables. For example, in a business environment facing economic uncertainty, leaders might plan for scenarios where demand fluctuates significantly, supply chains are disrupted, or regulatory changes impact operations. By having contingency strategies in place, leaders can respond more quickly and effectively when these uncertainties materialize.

In addition to scenario planning, leaders should also develop flexible strategies that can adapt to changing circumstances. In uncertain environments, rigid plans are often less effective because they cannot accommodate unexpected developments. Instead, leaders should focus on creating strategies that allow for quick pivots and adjustments as new information becomes available. This flexibility is key to thriving in the pressure cooker of decision-making under uncertainty.

Trusting Your Team: Empowering Others to Make Decisions

In high-stakes scenarios, the pressure to make the right decision often falls squarely on the shoulders of senior leaders. However, effective leadership is not about making every decision single-handedly. Instead, it's about empowering others within the organization to take ownership of decisions and contribute to the problem-solving process.

Delegating decision-making authority can alleviate the burden on leaders and promote a more agile and responsive organization. When team members are trusted to make decisions within their areas of expertise, it not only speeds up the decision-making process but also fosters a sense of accountability and ownership. Moreover, empowering teams allows leaders to tap into a wider range of perspectives and ideas, leading to more creative and well-rounded solutions.

To successfully delegate decision-making, leaders must cultivate a culture of trust and provide the necessary resources and support for their teams to succeed. This includes clear communication of goals and expectations, as well as ongoing feedback and guidance. Leaders should also be willing to accept that mistakes may occur, and when they do, use them as learning opportunities rather than placing blame. By building a culture of trust and empowerment, leaders can create a more resilient organization that thrives under pressure.

Tools for Quick, Effective Decision-Making

In today's fast-paced business environment, leaders and organizations often find themselves in situations where swift decisions are critical. The ability to make quick, yet effective, decisions can be the difference between success and failure, especially in high-pressure or crisis scenarios. However, rapid decision-making does not imply rushed or uninformed choices. Instead, it involves leveraging a range of tools and frameworks that allow for speed while maintaining clarity, accuracy, and foresight.

In this chapter, we explore several essential tools and techniques for making quick and effective decisions, each designed to help leaders navigate complexity, manage uncertainty, and drive actionable outcomes. These tools range from intuitive decision-making strategies to data-driven methodologies, ensuring that leaders can adapt to various situations and make the best possible choices, even under tight time constraints.

1. The OODA Loop: Observe, Orient, Decide, and Act

The OODA Loop, developed by military strategist John Boyd, is a decision-making framework that emphasizes speed and agility. It is particularly effective in environments where conditions are constantly changing and decisions must be made quickly to maintain a competitive advantage. The four steps of the OODA Loop—Observe, Orient, Decide, and Act—can be applied in various business scenarios, from launching new products to responding to crises.

- Observe: The first step is to gather as much relevant information as possible about the current situation. In a business context, this might involve collecting market data, customer feedback, or insights from team members. The key is to quickly understand what is happening without getting bogged down by excessive detail.

- Orient: Once the relevant data is collected, the next step is to interpret it in the context of your environment. This is where experience, intuition, and understanding of the broader market come into play. For example, if a company notices a sudden drop in sales, they might orient themselves by considering external factors such as economic downturns, changes in consumer behavior, or competitive actions.

- Decide: After interpreting the information, the next step is to make a decision. This is where many decision-makers get stuck, fearing the consequences of a wrong choice. However, the OODA Loop encourages leaders to make decisions quickly, knowing that they can always adjust based on new information.

- Act: Finally, the decision must be implemented. The faster you act on your decision, the sooner you can observe the outcomes and adjust your strategy if necessary. The cyclical nature of the OODA Loop means that after acting, you immediately return to the observation phase, continuously refining your approach based on the latest data.

Example: A retail chain using the OODA Loop might observe an unexpected surge in demand for a particular product. They quickly orient themselves by analyzing sales trends, supply chain capabilities, and competitor offerings. Based on this, they decide to increase their stock of the product and adjust their marketing efforts. After acting, they observe customer responses and sales data, allowing them to further refine their strategy in real-time.

2. Eisenhower Matrix: Prioritizing Urgency and Importance

One of the most common challenges in quick decision-making is determining what to focus on. The Eisenhower Matrix, also known as the Urgent-Important Matrix, helps decision-makers prioritize tasks by categorizing them into four quadrants:

1. Urgent and Important: Tasks that require immediate attention and have significant consequences.

2. Not Urgent but Important: Tasks that are important for long-term success but don't require immediate action.

3. Urgent but Not Important: Tasks that need immediate attention but don't contribute significantly to long-term goals.

4. Not Urgent and Not Important: Tasks that are neither urgent nor important and should be minimized or eliminated.

By using this matrix, leaders can quickly decide where to direct their time and energy, focusing on tasks that drive meaningful outcomes rather than getting distracted by low-priority issues.

Example: A startup CEO facing a product launch might use the Eisenhower Matrix to prioritize their efforts. Meeting with key investors (urgent and important) takes precedence over reviewing social media engagement (urgent but not important). Meanwhile, long-term strategy planning (not urgent but important) gets scheduled for later, ensuring that no critical tasks are overlooked.

3. The 80/20 Rule (Pareto Principle)

The 80/20 Rule, also known as the Pareto Principle, is a powerful tool for decision-making under pressure. It suggests that 80% of results often come from 20% of efforts. By identifying and focusing on the 20% of actions that generate the most significant impact, leaders can make quicker, more effective decisions without being overwhelmed by the need to address every possible issue.

This principle is particularly useful in business situations where resources—whether time, money, or manpower—are limited, and decisions need to be made about where to allocate them most effectively.

Example: A marketing team working on a campaign might realize that 80% of their sales come from 20% of their customer base. By focusing their efforts on nurturing relationships with these key customers, they can achieve better results without wasting time and resources on less impactful segments of their audience.

4. Decision Trees: Mapping Out Outcomes

A decision tree is a visual representation of possible choices and their potential outcomes. It allows decision-makers to map out different courses of action and evaluate the risks and benefits associated with each. By breaking down complex decisions into smaller, manageable components, decision trees enable quick and logical decision-making.

Example: A software company deciding whether to develop a new feature might create a decision tree outlining the potential costs, development time, and market demand for different options. Each branch of the tree represents a different decision path, with outcomes such as increased user engagement, higher revenue, or potential technical challenges. By visually comparing these scenarios, the team can quickly determine the most viable option.

5. SWOT Analysis: Assessing Strengths, Weaknesses, Opportunities, and Threats

SWOT analysis is a tool used to evaluate the internal and external factors affecting a decision. By analyzing an organization's strengths, weaknesses, opportunities, and threats, leaders can gain a holistic view of the situation and make informed decisions that capitalize on strengths and opportunities while mitigating risks associated with weaknesses and threats.

Example: A company considering an international expansion might use a SWOT analysis to evaluate its position. Strengths might include a strong brand reputation and existing global partnerships, while weaknesses could involve limited local market knowledge. Opportunities could include untapped markets and favorable trade agreements, while threats might involve regulatory challenges or cultural differences. This analysis helps the company quickly assess whether the expansion is a wise move and what potential hurdles it must address.

6. The Five Whys: Root Cause Analysis

The Five Whys technique is a simple yet effective tool for identifying the root cause of a problem. By asking "why" five times, decision-makers can drill down to the underlying issue, rather than simply addressing symptoms. This approach ensures that decisions are based on addressing the core problem, leading to more sustainable solutions.

Example: A manufacturing company experiencing a drop in production efficiency might use the Five Whys to identify the root cause. The first "why" might reveal that machines are malfunctioning. The second "why" could uncover that maintenance schedules have been neglected. The third "why" might point to staff shortages in the maintenance department, and so on. By the fifth "why," the company identifies a lack of proper training as the core issue and can address it directly, leading to a more effective solution.

7. Rapid Prototyping and Testing: Fail Fast, Learn Faster

In fast-moving industries, particularly in tech and product development, rapid prototyping and testing are essential tools for decision-making. Rather than spending months or years developing a product or service before launching it, companies can use rapid prototyping to create a minimum viable product (MVP) and test it with real users. The feedback gathered during this testing phase helps leaders make quick, informed decisions about whether to continue, pivot, or abandon the project.

Example: A tech startup developing a new mobile app might release an MVP to a small group of users, gathering feedback on usability, features, and potential improvements. Based on this feedback, the team can make quick decisions about which features to prioritize, which to cut, and how to improve the overall user experience before a full-scale launch.

8. RACI Matrix: Clarifying Roles and Responsibilities

When quick decisions need to be made, confusion about roles and responsibilities can slow down the process. The RACI Matrix is a tool used to clarify who is Responsible, Accountable, Consulted, and Informed in decision-making processes. By assigning clear roles to each team member, the RACI Matrix ensures that decisions are made efficiently and that the right people are involved at the right time.

Example: In a project to roll out a new software system across a company, the RACI Matrix might designate the IT manager as Responsible for implementation, the CEO as Accountable for the decision to proceed, key department heads as Consulted for input, and the entire staff as Informed once the decision is made. This structure streamlines the decision-making process by ensuring everyone knows their role.

9. Heuristics: Leveraging Mental Shortcuts

Heuristics are mental shortcuts or "rules of thumb" that help decision-makers quickly arrive at solutions based on past experiences and general patterns. While heuristics can sometimes lead to bias, they are useful for making quick decisions when time is of the essence. The key is knowing when to rely on heuristics and when to dig deeper into data or analysis.

Example: A seasoned sales manager might use the "80

/20 rule" as a heuristic, knowing that 80% of sales often come from 20% of clients. When faced with time constraints, the manager might prioritize meetings with the top 20% of clients, trusting that this will lead to the best results, rather than spending equal time on lower-priority accounts.

Quick, effective decision-making is essential in today's fast-paced world, where opportunities can vanish as quickly as they appear. By utilizing tools like the OODA Loop, Eisenhower Matrix, SWOT Analysis, and Decision Trees, leaders can ensure that their decisions are not only swift but also well-informed and strategically sound. Each tool offers a different approach to navigating complexity, managing risks, and making the best use of available resources. With these tools in hand, decision-makers can confidently tackle the challenges that come their way, ensuring that their organizations stay agile, competitive, and poised for success.

Decision-Making Tool	Key Focus	Purpose	Speed/Time Efficiency	Example Scenario
OODA Loop	Speed and adaptability	Make quick decisions in dynamic environments	High	Retail chain adjusting to market demands based on real-time sales data
Eisenhower Matrix	Prioritization of urgency and importance	Categorize tasks to focus on what matters most	Medium	Prioritizing investor meetings over social media reviews in a startup
80/20 Rule (Pareto)	Identifying high-impact actions	Focus on the 20% of efforts that generate 80% of results	High	Marketing team targeting 20% of customers generating most sales
Decision Trees	Mapping decision outcomes	Evaluate risks and rewards of different options	Medium	Software company deciding between feature development paths based on potential outcomes
SWOT Analysis	Internal and external environment evaluation	Assess strengths, weaknesses, opportunities, and threats	Medium	A company evaluating international expansion opportunities
Five Whys	Root cause identification	Drill down to the core issue of a problem	High	Manufacturing firm identifying the root cause of a production drop-off

Rapid Prototyping	Iterative product testing	Quickly test and adapt products in real-world scenarios	High	Tech startup testing a minimum viable product (MVP) for user feedback
RACI Matrix	Clarification of roles and responsibilities	Define clear roles in decision-making processes	High	Software rollout project designating who is responsible and accountable for each step
Heuristics	Mental shortcuts based on experience	Make quick decisions using "rules of thumb"	High	Sales manager focusing on the top 20% of clients based on past sales patterns

CHAPTER 2: STRATEGIC PIVOT POINTS: WHEN TO CHANGE COURSE AND WHY

In the life of any business, there are critical moments that can define its future success or failure. These moments are often marked by the need for a strategic pivot—a deliberate shift in direction to align with new realities, opportunities, or challenges. But how does a leader recognize when it's time to change course? What are the signals that indicate a need for reevaluation, and more importantly, why is it crucial to pivot at the right moment?

Recognizing Key Moments for Change

Business environments are dynamic, constantly evolving landscapes shaped by technological advancements, shifting consumer preferences, regulatory changes, competitive pressures, and macroeconomic trends. In this ever-changing world, the ability to identify when a course correction is necessary is a hallmark of strong leadership. Successful business leaders know that even the best-laid plans can become outdated in the face of new information. The key is recognizing the subtle (and sometimes not-so-subtle) signals that it's time to pivot before it's too late.

One of the most obvious indicators that a strategic pivot may be necessary is stagnation or declining performance. When growth slows or revenue plateaus, it's often a sign that the current strategy is no longer aligned with the market. However, it's important to note that this recognition must go beyond short-term fluctuations or seasonal changes. Leaders need to adopt a broader perspective, looking at long-term trends and patterns. If, for example, a business has seen consistent growth for several years but is now facing a steady decline in market share, it's crucial to question whether the current strategy still fits the evolving marketplace.

It's not only negative signals that should prompt a pivot. Sometimes, rapid growth or unexpected success can also be an indication that a change in direction is needed. When a company experiences unexpected demand or sees its market expand faster than anticipated, it may need to pivot to take full advantage of the opportunity. This could involve scaling operations, expanding product lines, or shifting focus to new customer segments. In these instances, a pivot is about maximizing potential rather than correcting course.

Equally important are external factors such as disruptive technologies, competitor innovation, or regulatory shifts. Companies that are too focused on their internal metrics may miss these external warning signs. Consider how the rise of digital photography disrupted the traditional film industry, or how streaming services upended cable television. Companies that failed to recognize these external shifts were left behind, while those that pivoted quickly, such as Netflix's move from DVD rentals to streaming, thrived. Being tuned into both industry-specific and broader technological trends allows businesses to anticipate shifts rather than simply react to them.

The feedback from customers is another critical factor in recognizing when it's time to pivot. The best companies maintain an open dialogue with their customers, actively seeking out feedback and incorporating it into their strategic decisions. Declining customer satisfaction, an increase in complaints, or a shift in customer preferences can all be strong indicators that it's time to reconsider the current strategy. Listening to customers is not just about addressing individual complaints; it's about understanding the broader trends and patterns that may signal a need for change.

But recognizing the need for a pivot is only half the battle. Once the signals have been identified, leaders must then make the difficult decision to change course. This is often easier said than done. Businesses are built on momentum, and changing direction can feel like abandoning a well-worn path. There may be emotional and financial investments tied to the current strategy, and the fear of the unknown can be paralyzing. Yet, inaction can be far more dangerous. The history of business is littered with examples of companies that failed to pivot when they needed to and paid the price. Kodak, Blockbuster, and Nokia are just a few names that come to mind.

Pivoting, therefore, is not about abandoning what works but recognizing that what worked in the past may not necessarily work in the future. The ability to pivot requires a combination of humility, foresight, and courage—humility to acknowledge that the current strategy may no longer be the right one, foresight to anticipate future trends, and courage to take bold actions in the face of uncertainty.

The Why Behind Strategic Pivots

So why is it so critical to pivot at the right time? The answer lies in the very nature of business evolution. Markets change, competitors adapt, and consumer behaviors shift. A company that fails to evolve alongside these changes risks becoming obsolete. The business world is littered with companies that once dominated their industries but failed to pivot when the time came.

One of the most compelling reasons for a strategic pivot is the need to stay ahead of competition. In highly competitive markets, the companies that succeed are often those that can anticipate changes and respond to them faster than their rivals. A well-timed pivot can not only help a company maintain its competitive edge but can also position it as a market leader. For example, when Apple recognized that the future of personal computing lay in mobile devices rather than desktop computers, it pivoted towards developing the iPhone. This strategic pivot didn't just keep Apple competitive—it made it a global leader in technology.

Another reason for a strategic pivot is to avoid the sunk cost fallacy—the tendency to continue investing in a failing course of action because of the resources already committed. Leaders must have the discipline to detach from past investments and recognize when those investments no longer serve the company's future. As hard as it may be, sometimes cutting losses and redirecting resources to new opportunities is the best course of action.

A strategic pivot can also be driven by the need to innovate and stay relevant. In today's fast-paced world, innovation is not just a competitive advantage—it's a necessity for survival. Companies that cling to outdated products, services, or business models risk being overtaken by more innovative competitors. By embracing a pivot, companies can explore new technologies, business models, or market segments, breathing fresh life into the organization. Consider the example of IBM, which pivoted from a hardware company to a services and software provider, ensuring its continued relevance in the tech industry.

Pivots are also essential in responding to macroeconomic shifts. Globalization, economic downturns, and political instability can all create new risks and opportunities for businesses. Companies that are able to pivot their strategies in response to these macroeconomic factors are better positioned to survive and thrive in uncertain environments. During the 2008 financial crisis, many companies had to pivot their business models to adapt to the new economic reality. Some moved towards leaner operations, while others diversified their revenue streams to reduce risk. These strategic pivots allowed companies to weather the storm and emerge stronger on the other side.

Timing, of course, is everything. A pivot that is executed too early may miss the full potential of the current strategy, while one that is too late may result in missed opportunities or irreversible damage. The best leaders are those who can navigate this delicate balance, understanding when to stay the course and when to change direction.

How to Pivot Successfully

While recognizing the need to pivot is crucial, executing the pivot effectively is where the real challenge lies. A successful pivot requires a clear vision of where the company is heading and a well-thought-out strategy for getting there. This often involves making tough decisions, such as reallocating resources, restructuring teams, or even exiting certain markets. The pivot must be communicated clearly to all stakeholders, ensuring that everyone is aligned with the new direction.

One of the most important aspects of a successful pivot is maintaining flexibility. The new strategy should be adaptable, allowing the company to make further adjustments as needed. This requires a culture that encourages experimentation and is open to failure. Not every pivot will succeed, but the ability to learn from mistakes and iterate quickly is what separates successful companies from those that falter.

Additionally, a pivot should be customer-centric. Ultimately, the success of any strategic shift will depend on how well it serves the needs of the customer. Businesses that pivot without considering their customers risk alienating their base and losing market share. This is why it's so important to involve customers in the pivot process—through feedback, focus groups, or beta testing new products or services.

Finally, a successful pivot requires strong leadership. Leaders must be able to rally their teams around the new vision, providing the direction and support needed to execute the pivot. This includes fostering a sense of urgency, managing resistance to change, and ensuring that the organization has the resources and capabilities needed to succeed in the new direction.

Strategic pivot points are inevitable in the life of any business. Recognizing when to change course and understanding why that change is necessary are critical skills for any business leader. Whether driven by declining performance, external disruption, or the need for innovation, a well-executed pivot can be the difference between stagnation and growth, between failure and success. The best leaders are those who can anticipate these pivot points and guide their organizations through them with clarity, courage, and conviction.

Case Studies of Successful and Failed Pivots

The ability to pivot effectively is a defining trait of many successful businesses. However, the path of strategic pivots is littered with both triumphs and failures. The following case studies offer insights into companies that managed to pivot successfully and those that faltered. Through examining both sides of the coin, we can learn valuable lessons about the dynamics of change, leadership, timing, and execution.

Successful Pivots

1. Netflix: From DVD Rentals to Streaming

Netflix provides one of the most well-known and successful examples of a strategic pivot in modern business history. Founded in 1997 as a DVD rental service, Netflix initially capitalized on the inconvenience of traditional video rental stores like Blockbuster, offering customers the ability to order DVDs online and receive them by mail. Netflix's original business model was innovative, but the company's leaders, including CEO Reed Hastings, saw the writing on the wall when digital media began to grow in popularity.

By the mid-2000s, broadband internet was becoming more widespread, and the rise of streaming technology presented both a challenge and an opportunity for Netflix. Hastings and his team realized that the future of content consumption would be digital, so they made the bold decision to pivot away from physical DVD rentals and focus on streaming. This was a radical shift, particularly because Netflix's DVD-by-mail service was still highly profitable at the time.

The pivot to streaming was a risk. It required substantial investment in technology infrastructure, content licensing, and the development of a new user experience. In addition, it meant competing against emerging digital platforms like Hulu and the looming threat of tech giants such as Amazon. Nonetheless, the company understood that clinging to its DVD business would lead to eventual obsolescence.

The shift to streaming was hugely successful, not only enabling Netflix to survive but allowing it to dominate the entertainment industry. The company's focus on original content, beginning with House of Cards in 2013, further cemented its position as a market leader. Today, Netflix has over 230 million subscribers globally, and its decision to pivot early and decisively was key to its rise as a major player in the media landscape. The lesson here is clear: Netflix's leaders understood when to make the hard decision to abandon a profitable model in favor of long-term growth, and they executed the pivot with clear vision and strategy.

2. Starbucks: From Coffee Beans to Coffeehouse Experience

In its early days, Starbucks was primarily a retailer of coffee beans and equipment. When Howard Schultz first joined the company as Director of Retail Operations and Marketing in 1982, he visited Italy and was inspired by the vibrant coffee culture he saw there. He noted that Italian coffee bars were not just about the coffee itself but the experience of socializing, relaxing, and spending time in a comfortable environment. Schultz saw an opportunity to bring that culture to the United States, and when his initial suggestion to create espresso bars within Starbucks stores was met with resistance, he eventually left the company to start his own coffeehouse venture.

After realizing Schultz's success with his coffee bars, Starbucks' original owners invited him back to lead the company, and Schultz executed a strategic pivot that would change the course of Starbucks forever. Rather than being a place that sold coffee beans, Starbucks shifted to becoming a destination for high-quality coffee beverages served in an inviting, community-oriented atmosphere.

This pivot transformed Starbucks into a global brand synonymous with coffee culture. Schultz's vision of creating a "third place" between home and work resonated with consumers, and the company's focus on customer experience—comfortable seating, friendly baristas, and personalized drink orders—became its hallmark. The pivot enabled Starbucks to expand from a small chain of stores in Seattle to a global empire with over 35,000 locations worldwide.

The success of Starbucks' pivot lies in Schultz's ability to recognize not just a change in consumer behavior but an opportunity to create a new experience around a product. Starbucks didn't just sell coffee; it sold an experience, a social environment that people wanted to be part of. This pivot illustrates how businesses can grow exponentially by not only improving their product but by transforming how that product is consumed.

3. Slack: From Failed Video Game to Communication Powerhouse

Slack's origin story is another testament to the power of pivoting in response to market conditions. Before it became a ubiquitous workplace communication tool, Slack was part of a company called Tiny Speck, which was working on a massively multiplayer online game called Glitch. Despite significant investment and a dedicated development team, Glitch failed to attract a substantial audience. Faced with the game's failure, Tiny Speck was forced to shut it down.

Instead of folding entirely, Stewart Butterfield, the CEO of Tiny Speck, realized that one of the tools they had developed for internal communication while working on Glitch had immense potential. That tool was Slack. Butterfield and his team had created an internal messaging system to coordinate between remote team members, allowing for more seamless communication than traditional email. They recognized that other companies might benefit from this type of tool, especially as more businesses were shifting towards distributed teams.

Tiny Speck pivoted away from game development and focused on turning Slack into a product that could be marketed to other businesses. This pivot was highly successful, with Slack growing into one of the most widely used business communication platforms in the world. In 2021, Salesforce acquired Slack for $27.7 billion, cementing its place as a key player in the future of work.

The lesson here is that even when a business seems to be failing, there may be hidden assets or opportunities that can serve as the foundation for a successful pivot. Slack's pivot demonstrates the importance of flexibility, creativity, and the willingness to recognize value in unexpected places.

Failed Pivots

1. Kodak: The Missed Opportunity in Digital Photography

Kodak, once a titan of the photography industry, offers a cautionary tale of what happens when a company fails to pivot at a critical moment. For much of the 20th century, Kodak dominated the film photography market, with its brand becoming synonymous with taking pictures. However, in the 1980s and 1990s, digital photography began to emerge, threatening the very foundation of Kodak's business model, which was heavily reliant on film sales.

Ironically, Kodak was one of the first companies to invent digital photography technology. In 1975, a Kodak engineer developed the first digital camera, but Kodak's leadership was hesitant to embrace it. The company feared that digital photography would cannibalize its highly profitable film business, so it focused on protecting the status quo rather than embracing the future.

By the time Kodak finally decided to enter the digital photography market, it was too late. Competitors like Sony and Canon had already captured significant market share, and consumer preferences had shifted towards digital. Despite several attempts to pivot—most notably by moving into digital cameras and online photo-sharing services—Kodak's efforts were half-hearted and came too late. The company filed for bankruptcy in 2012.

Kodak's failure to pivot highlights the dangers of clinging to a profitable business model while ignoring disruptive technologies. The company's leadership underestimated the speed and impact of the digital revolution and failed to invest in the future until it was too late. The lesson here is clear: even dominant companies must be willing to disrupt themselves before competitors do it for them.

2. Blockbuster: The Netflix That Never Was

Blockbuster is another classic example of a company that failed to pivot when it mattered most. In the early 2000s, Blockbuster was the king of video rentals, with thousands of stores around the world. However, as streaming services began to emerge, the company was slow to recognize the shift in consumer behavior. By the time Netflix introduced its DVD-by-mail service and then moved into streaming, Blockbuster was still clinging to its brick-and-mortar model.

One of the most significant moments in Blockbuster's history was in 2000 when Netflix offered to sell itself to Blockbuster for $50 million. Blockbuster turned down the offer, believing that its traditional rental model was still the future of home entertainment. This decision proved disastrous, as Netflix quickly gained traction with consumers who preferred the convenience of streaming over visiting a physical store.

Blockbuster eventually tried to pivot by launching its own online rental service, but by that point, Netflix had already established itself as the leader in the space. The pivot came too late, and Blockbuster could not recover. In 2010, Blockbuster filed for bankruptcy, and today, only one Blockbuster store remains open as a nostalgic relic of a bygone era.

Blockbuster's failure to pivot underscores the importance of being proactive rather than reactive. The company's leadership was overly confident in its existing business model and failed to recognize the disruptive potential of streaming. The lesson here is that pivots must be timely and forward-looking. Failing to recognize changes in consumer behavior or technological trends can lead to irrelevance and ultimately, failure.

3. BlackBerry: The Fall from Mobile Dominance

In the early 2000s, BlackBerry was the dominant player in the smartphone market, particularly among business professionals. Its iconic physical keyboard and secure email service made it the device of choice for corporate users and government officials. However, when Apple introduced the iPhone in 2007, followed by Google's Android platform, the smartphone market began to shift dramatically towards touchscreens and app-based ecosystems.

BlackBerry's leadership initially dismissed the iPhone as a toy and believed that their focus on security and productivity would continue to give them an edge. However, as consumer preferences shifted towards more versatile, touchscreen-based devices, BlackBerry failed to pivot quickly enough. The company did eventually release touchscreen phones, but by then, it had lost significant market share to Apple and Android.

BlackBerry's failure to pivot was a result of its inability to foresee how consumer preferences would evolve and its over-reliance on its business-oriented customer base. The lesson from BlackBerry's downfall is that companies need to be aware of changes in both technology and consumer behavior. BlackBerry's slow response to the iPhone allowed its competitors to dominate the smartphone market, and the company has since faded into relative obscurity.

The ability to pivot successfully is a critical skill for any business, especially in today's rapidly evolving marketplace. The success stories of Netflix, Starbucks, and Slack show that with the right timing, foresight, and execution, companies can not only survive but thrive by adapting to new market realities. Conversely, the failures of Kodak, Blockbuster, and BlackBerry serve as stark reminders of the dangers of clinging to outdated business models and underestimating the impact of technological disruption.

Ultimately, the key to a successful pivot lies in the willingness to embrace change, even when it means sacrificing short-term profitability for long-term survival. Companies that recognize opportunities, remain agile, and are willing to disrupt themselves are more likely to succeed, while those that resist change risk being left behind in an increasingly competitive landscape.

1. How can you ensure that your business is constantly scanning for emerging trends and potential disruptions, and what steps would you take to pivot early enough to stay ahead of the competition?

2. Reflecting on the failures of Kodak, Blockbuster, and BlackBerry, what lessons can you apply to your own business decisions to avoid being complacent with your current success?

3. When considering a strategic pivot, how do you balance the risks of abandoning a profitable business model with the potential long-term gains of embracing innovation?

Reflection Question	Key Insights / Suggested Approach
How can you ensure that your business is constantly scanning for emerging trends and potential disruptions, and what steps would you take to pivot early enough to stay ahead of the competition?	Implement regular market analysis and trend monitoring; foster a culture of innovation and flexibility. Empower leadership teams to identify early warning signs of disruption and encourage proactive strategy discussions to consider pivot opportunities.
Reflecting on the failures of Kodak, Blockbuster, and BlackBerry, what lessons can you apply to your own business decisions to avoid being complacent with your current success?	Avoid complacency by continuously innovating, even when the current model is successful. Recognize the importance of adapting to consumer behavior and technological advances. Learn from past failures by staying agile and being willing to disrupt yourself.
When considering a strategic pivot, how do you balance the risks of abandoning a profitable business model with the potential long-term gains of embracing innovation?	Weigh the potential loss of short-term profitability against future market opportunities. Evaluate both internal capabilities and external forces. Create a detailed roadmap that minimizes disruption while embracing innovation for sustainable growth.

CHAPTER 3: LEADING THROUGH CRISIS: TURNING CHALLENGES INTO OPPORTUNITIES

In the fast-paced and unpredictable world of business, crises are inevitable. Whether due to external disruptions like economic downturns, technological shifts, or internal conflicts like leadership transitions or financial instability, every organization will face moments that test its resolve. The true hallmark of an effective leader is not the ability to avoid crises but the skill to navigate them with foresight, poise, and strategy. A crisis, though fraught with challenges, also presents unique opportunities for innovation, growth, and reinvention. This chapter delves into the frameworks that help leaders transform crises from daunting threats into pivotal moments of opportunity.

Crisis Leadership Frameworks

Understanding crisis leadership is about more than just reactive problem-solving. It requires the adoption of strategic frameworks that enable leaders to respond effectively to the complexities of high-stakes situations. These frameworks act as structured roadmaps, offering guiding principles and methods to assess, respond, and thrive amid uncertainty. Below, we explore several widely recognized crisis leadership frameworks that help organizations not only survive crises but emerge stronger.

1. The Adaptive Leadership Framework

Adaptive leadership, first introduced by Harvard professors Ronald Heifetz and Marty Linsky, is particularly relevant during times of crisis. This framework emphasizes flexibility, learning, and collaboration, requiring leaders to pivot from traditional authoritative approaches to more fluid, dynamic strategies.

- Diagnose the Situation: Before responding to a crisis, leaders must accurately assess the scope and depth of the problem. Is the crisis technical (with clear solutions and known variables) or adaptive (complex, systemic, and ambiguous)? For adaptive challenges, traditional methods of problem-solving often fail. Leaders must prepare to rethink established assumptions and innovate beyond known solutions.

- Empower the Team: One of the cornerstones of adaptive leadership is encouraging distributed leadership. This means that in a crisis, decisions should not be made solely at the top. Instead, leaders should empower team members across all levels to take initiative, contribute ideas, and act. This decentralization fosters agility and creativity, essential traits in a rapidly shifting crisis scenario.

- Learn and Adapt: Crises are inherently unpredictable. The best leaders use crises as opportunities for learning, continually adapting their strategies as new information emerges. In this sense, leadership is less about having all the answers and more about fostering a culture of experimentation, reflection, and learning.

2. The Situational Leadership Framework

Developed by Paul Hersey and Ken Blanchard, situational leadership is based on the premise that there is no one-size-fits-all approach to leadership. Instead, effective leaders adapt their style based on the demands of the situation and the readiness level of their team members. This model is particularly valuable during crises when the team may experience heightened stress, uncertainty, and varying degrees of motivation.

- Assess the Readiness of Team Members: In a crisis, team members may react differently—some may be confident and ready to take charge, while others may feel overwhelmed and need additional support. Leaders must assess the team's readiness to determine the most appropriate leadership style. Are they competent but lacking confidence? Are they inexperienced but enthusiastic? These factors dictate the leader's response.

- Adjust Leadership Style: Depending on the situation and the team's readiness, leaders must adjust their approach:

  - Directing for team members who lack experience or are overwhelmed.

  - Coaching for those who need guidance but are motivated.

  - Supporting when team members have skills but lack confidence.

  - Delegating when the team is highly competent and confident in their roles.

In a crisis, using situational leadership helps ensure that each team member receives the guidance or autonomy they need to perform effectively. By aligning leadership style with the situation at hand, leaders can minimize stress and ensure a coordinated response to the crisis.

3. The Four-Stage Crisis Management Framework

This widely recognized framework breaks down crisis management into four stages: Mitigation, Preparedness, Response, and Recovery. It provides leaders with a comprehensive approach to managing crises before, during, and after they occur.

- Mitigation: This stage involves taking proactive steps to reduce the likelihood and impact of potential crises. Leaders must conduct risk assessments, identify vulnerabilities, and implement safeguards to minimize the impact of possible disruptions. This might include strengthening cybersecurity measures, diversifying supply chains, or investing in crisis communication training for staff.

- Preparedness: Despite mitigation efforts, crises will occur. Preparedness involves creating detailed crisis response plans, establishing clear communication channels, and training staff on their roles in a crisis. The goal is to ensure that when a crisis strikes, the organization is ready to act swiftly and effectively.

- Response: During the response phase, leaders must make quick, decisive actions to address the crisis. Key to this stage is clear, transparent communication—both internally with employees and externally with stakeholders. Leaders must also prioritize actions based on immediate needs, whether that's protecting employees, securing assets, or managing public relations.

- Recovery: Once the immediate crisis has been managed, leaders must focus on the recovery phase. This includes repairing any damage to the organization, whether financial, reputational, or operational. The recovery phase is also an opportunity to reflect on lessons learned and make improvements to crisis management plans for the future.

The Four-Stage Crisis Management Framework is an essential tool for any leader looking to guide their organization through the tumultuous waves of a crisis. By methodically preparing for and managing each stage of the crisis, leaders can minimize damage and expedite recovery.

4. The Five Leadership Roles in Crisis Framework

This framework, as articulated by Harvard's John P. Kotter, identifies five key roles that leaders must embody during a crisis. Each role serves a distinct purpose in ensuring that the organization not only survives but seizes the opportunity to innovate and grow.

- The Communicator: In times of crisis, leaders must be the voice of clarity and calm. This role involves keeping all stakeholders—employees, customers, shareholders—well-informed about the nature of the crisis and the steps being taken. Transparent, consistent communication is critical for maintaining trust and ensuring that everyone is aligned in their efforts.

- The Decision-Maker: A crisis often necessitates rapid decision-making under pressure. Leaders must be able to make tough, timely decisions based on incomplete information. The ability to balance speed with thoughtfulness is crucial in preventing a crisis from escalating further.

- The Visionary: While managing the immediate fallout of a crisis is essential, leaders must also look ahead to the future. The visionary role involves identifying the opportunities hidden within the crisis and using them to drive innovation and strategic change. For instance, the COVID-19 pandemic, while devastating, also prompted many companies to adopt digital technologies more rapidly than they might have otherwise.

- The Team Builder: Crises can strain even the most cohesive teams. It is the leader's job to foster a sense of unity and purpose during these difficult times. This involves not only rallying the team around a common goal but also ensuring that team members feel supported and valued throughout the process.

- The Learner: Finally, effective leaders are learners. They view each crisis as a chance to gather insights and improve for the future. Once the dust settles, it is important to reflect on what worked, what didn't, and how the organization can become more resilient moving forward.

Navigating a crisis requires more than just reactive decision-making; it demands a thoughtful, strategic approach. By adopting frameworks like Adaptive Leadership, Situational Leadership, and the Four-Stage Crisis Management model, leaders can create structured responses to chaotic situations, minimizing damage while maximizing opportunities for growth. Furthermore, by embracing roles like the Communicator, Decision-Maker, and Visionary, leaders can ensure that their organizations not only survive but thrive in the face of adversity.

Ultimately, crises are not simply threats—they are catalysts for change. With the right frameworks, leaders can transform these high-stakes moments into pivotal opportunities for innovation, adaptation, and long-term success.

How to Maintain Focus Under Pressure

Maintaining focus under pressure is one of the most critical skills in today's fast-paced world, whether in the context of high-stakes business scenarios, demanding academic environments, or personal life challenges. Pressure often leads to stress, which can impair decision-making, cloud judgment, and cause mental fatigue. However, those who master the art of staying focused in such situations not only survive but thrive, turning pressure into an opportunity for growth and achievement. This chapter delves into actionable strategies to maintain focus under pressure, illustrated with examples from business, sports, and psychology.

Understanding the Nature of Pressure

Before exploring strategies for maintaining focus, it is essential to first understand the nature of pressure. Pressure can arise from external circumstances, such as deadlines, expectations from stakeholders, or financial challenges. It can also be internally generated, stemming from perfectionism, fear of failure, or personal ambition. Recognizing the sources of pressure is the first step toward addressing them effectively.

Take, for example, a CEO of a growing tech startup facing the pressure of securing funding while simultaneously managing a team and ensuring product development stays on track. In this scenario, external pressures include investor demands and competitive market forces, while internal pressures may be rooted in the fear of disappointing investors or making decisions that could harm the company's future. Both types of pressure can cloud focus if not managed properly.

Strategy 1: Prioritization and Time Management

One of the most effective ways to maintain focus under pressure is through strategic prioritization and efficient time management. When faced with numerous tasks and responsibilities, it's easy to feel overwhelmed, which can lead to a scattered approach. The key is to identify the most critical tasks and allocate time and resources accordingly.

A clear example of this can be found in the lives of top executives like Tim Cook, CEO of Apple. Known for his extraordinary work ethic, Cook manages his time meticulously. He begins his day at 4:30 AM to focus on the most critical tasks before the rush of meetings and calls begin. By prioritizing the most important issues, Cook ensures that his focus is directed towards high-value tasks, even when faced with immense pressure from shareholders, employees, and customers.

Similarly, athletes like Serena Williams understand the value of prioritization when under pressure. During a Grand Slam tournament, her focus is singularly directed towards winning each match. Distractions are minimized, and her time is carefully structured around practice, rest, and mental preparation. In high-pressure moments, Williams' ability to maintain focus on the task at hand—whether it's serving under pressure or returning a crucial shot—is what sets her apart.

To implement prioritization in your own life or career, it helps to break down tasks into categories such as urgent, important, and non-essential. By focusing on tasks that fall into the first two categories, you can minimize the effects of pressure and direct your energy toward what truly matters.

Strategy 2: Mindfulness and Mental Conditioning

The ability to maintain focus under pressure is not just about managing time but also about managing one's mental state. Mindfulness and mental conditioning can be invaluable tools in this process. Practicing mindfulness allows individuals to stay present, avoid distractions, and prevent stress from overwhelming their focus.

In recent years, mindfulness has gained significant traction in corporate leadership. Executives from companies like Google, Salesforce, and LinkedIn incorporate mindfulness practices into their daily routines. Google's "Search Inside Yourself" program teaches employees how to manage stress, increase emotional intelligence, and remain calm under pressure through mindfulness and meditation. This program has proven particularly effective in helping individuals stay focused during high-pressure situations such as product launches, crises, or high-stakes negotiations.

A real-world example from sports involves NBA player LeBron James, who is known not only for his physical abilities but also for his mental focus during games. James practices mindfulness and meditation to center himself before high-pressure games, enabling him to maintain clarity and perform at his best, even during intense competition. His ability to focus under pressure is evident in his numerous game-winning shots, often made in the final seconds ofdwindling customer loyalty. Many leaders in Schultz's position might have crumbled under the weight of such immense pressure. However, Schultz approached the situation with a different mindset, using cognitive reframing to turn the crisis into an opportunity. Instead of viewing the financial downturn as a sign of failure, Schultz saw it as a chance to revitalize the brand. He focused on the core values that had initially driven Starbucks' success and implemented sweeping changes, including closing underperforming stores and refocusing on customer experience. His ability to reframe pressure as an opportunity allowed him to maintain focus and steer the company back to profitability.

Similarly, in personal challenges, cognitive reframing is key to maintaining focus under pressure. For example, students facing academic pressures during exams may feel overwhelmed by the fear of failure. However, by reframing the pressure as a sign of the importance of their work, they can shift their mindset from fear to motivation, using the pressure to fuel their performance rather than hinder it.

Positive thinking also plays a crucial role in maintaining focus. Athletes like Michael Jordan have spoken extensively about the power of positive self-talk and its impact on their performance under pressure. During the 1997 NBA Finals, Jordan was dealing with flu-like symptoms in Game 5—what later became known as "The Flu Game." Despite his physical limitations, Jordan's mental resilience and focus were unwavering. He maintained a positive mindset, telling himself that he could still contribute and lead his team. Jordan finished the game with 38 points, leading the Chicago Bulls to victory. His focus, despite the immense physical and mental pressure, is a testament to the power of cognitive reframing and positive thinking.

To apply cognitive reframing in your own life, try to identify situations where pressure makes you feel anxious or fearful, and then consciously reframe those feelings. Ask yourself, "What opportunity does this situation present? How can I use this pressure to perform better?" Over time, this practice will help build a mindset where pressure becomes synonymous with opportunity rather than stress.

Strategy 4: Developing a Clear Process and Rituals

Another critical way to maintain focus under pressure is by developing a clear process and creating personal rituals. When we are under pressure, uncertainty can often lead to distractions. However, by following a well-defined process and relying on habitual rituals, it becomes easier to stay focused and maintain consistency, even in the most chaotic circumstances.

In the business world, Jeff Bezos, founder of Amazon, is renowned for his ability to stay focused during high-stress moments. Bezos follows a consistent decision-making process where he distinguishes between "Type 1" and "Type 2" decisions. Type 1 decisions are irreversible and require careful deliberation, while Type 2 decisions are more easily reversible and can be made quickly. This mental framework allows him to maintain focus, even when faced with pressure to make swift, critical decisions. By relying on a clear process, Bezos minimizes the mental toll of pressure and ensures he is focused on making the best decisions for Amazon.

Rituals also play an important role in maintaining focus under pressure. Take the example of top athletes like tennis star Rafael Nadal. Nadal is famous for his meticulous pre-match rituals, which include how he arranges his water bottles and his precise routine when preparing to serve. These seemingly small rituals help him stay focused and block out external distractions during high-stakes matches. For Nadal, these rituals create a sense of control and predictability, even when the pressure on the court is at its highest.

Creating a process or ritual can be as simple as developing a morning routine that sets the tone for the day or establishing a specific pre-meeting checklist to ensure you're fully prepared. These small habits can anchor your focus and provide a sense of calm in the midst of pressure.

Strategy 5: Building Emotional Resilience

Maintaining focus under pressure is closely linked to emotional resilience—the ability to bounce back from setbacks and stay composed in stressful situations. Resilience is not something we are born with; it is a skill that can be developed through practice and experience.

Consider the example of Oprah Winfrey, one of the most successful media moguls in history. Throughout her career, Winfrey has faced numerous challenges, from growing up in poverty to experiencing public failures in her early career. However, she has consistently demonstrated emotional resilience by not allowing these setbacks to derail her focus. Instead, she views them as learning experiences and opportunities for growth. Winfrey's ability to remain focused in the face of adversity has been a critical factor in her long-term success.

Resilience is also critical for entrepreneurs, who often face significant pressures to deliver results despite uncertain conditions. Take Elon Musk, for example, who faced extreme pressure during the early years of SpaceX and Tesla. At one point, both companies were on the brink of failure, with SpaceX experiencing multiple failed rocket launches and Tesla facing financial difficulties. Musk, known for his high-pressure leadership style, remained focused on his long-term vision. His resilience allowed him to push through these challenges, ultimately leading SpaceX to successful launches and Tesla to become a major player in the electric vehicle market.

Building emotional resilience starts with understanding that setbacks and failures are a natural part of any high-pressure situation. Rather than dwelling on failures, resilient individuals focus on solutions, stay committed to their long-term goals, and view challenges as opportunities to improve. Developing a growth mindset—where you see every challenge as a learning opportunity—helps maintain focus and prevents pressure from overwhelming you.

Strategy 6: Physical Health and Well-Being

Physical health is often overlooked in discussions about maintaining focus under pressure, yet it plays a vital role in our cognitive abilities and stress management. Ensuring that you are physically fit, well-rested, and maintaining a healthy diet can dramatically improve your ability to focus, particularly in high-pressure environments.

Research has shown that physical exercise is one of the most effective ways to reduce stress and enhance focus. Business leaders like Richard Branson and Barack Obama have spoken openly about the importance of regular exercise in their routines. Branson, for instance, attributes much of his productivity and focus to daily physical activity, whether it's swimming, cycling, or tennis. In high-pressure situations, exercise helps release endorphins, improve mental clarity, and reduce the stress hormones that can impede focus.

Sleep is another crucial factor. Studies show that sleep deprivation impairs cognitive function, making it more difficult to concentrate and make decisions. Arianna Huffington, founder of the Huffington Post, experienced firsthand the dangers of neglecting sleep in a high-pressure environment. After collapsing from exhaustion in her office, she became a vocal advocate for the importance of sleep in maintaining productivity and focus. Her personal experience highlights how poor physical health can lead to mental burnout and diminished focus, especially when under pressure.

To maintain focus, it is essential to prioritize your physical well-being. This includes not only regular exercise and proper sleep but also staying hydrated, eating a balanced diet, and taking short breaks throughout the day to recharge. These habits contribute to a clearer mind and greater capacity to focus, even when faced with intense pressure.

Mastering Focus Under Pressure

Maintaining focus under pressure is a skill that can be developed through practice, resilience, and the implementation of effective strategies. By prioritizing tasks, practicing mindfulness, reframing cognitive challenges, establishing clear processes, building emotional resilience, and taking care of physical health, individuals can thrive in high-pressure environments. Whether you are a business leader facing a crisis, an athlete competing at the highest level, or an individual navigating personal challenges, the ability to remain focused will determine your success.

Pressure, while inevitable, does not have to be a hindrance. With the right mindset and tools, it can become the catalyst for growth, innovation, and peak performance.

CHAPTER 4: NAVIGATING CONFLICT: MANAGING STAKEHOLDERS AND COMPETING INTERESTS

In the high-stakes world of business, conflict is inevitable. Whether it's between teams, departments, or external stakeholders, navigating these conflicts effectively is crucial for any leader. How a leader manages these tensions will determine the success of not only individual projects but the overall health and sustainability of the organization. This chapter delves into the art of conflict resolution, offering proven strategies that empower business leaders to manage stakeholder relationships and balance competing interests with both authority and empathy.

Understanding the Nature of Conflict in Business

Conflicts arise for a variety of reasons: differences in goals, misaligned expectations, limited resources, or simply the clash of personalities. The key is not to avoid conflict, but to approach it as an opportunity for growth and innovation. When handled correctly, conflict can lead to more robust decision-making, stronger relationships, and improved team cohesion.

It is essential to understand that not all conflicts are equal. Some may involve internal stakeholders, such as employees and managers, while others could involve external parties, such as customers, suppliers, or regulators. The stakes, interests, and emotions at play can vary significantly depending on the parties involved. A one-size-fits-all approach will not suffice, and this is where strategic, nuanced conflict resolution skills come into play.

Conflict as a Catalyst for Innovation

While conflict is often perceived negatively, in the business context, it can serve as a powerful catalyst for innovation. When stakeholders disagree, it forces them to reevaluate their positions, test their assumptions, and explore alternatives. Often, the friction that comes from these disagreements is the very force that sparks creative problem-solving.

For example, in product development, tension between the marketing team (seeking to meet consumer demands) and the engineering team (focusing on technical feasibility) can lead to a more balanced product that is both marketable and functional. Without such a conflict, businesses run the risk of delivering products that either lack user appeal or technical soundness.

For conflict to result in innovation, it must be managed constructively. This requires leaders to foster a culture where differing opinions are encouraged, but where debate is structured, respectful, and goal-oriented.

The Role of the Leader in Conflict Resolution

As a leader, your role in conflict resolution is multifaceted. Not only are you a mediator between conflicting parties, but you are also a strategist who ensures that all interests are aligned with the overarching goals of the organization. Leaders must exhibit emotional intelligence, staying calm under pressure, actively listening to all parties, and identifying solutions that are win-win whenever possible.

Moreover, leaders must be skilled in recognizing the early signs of conflict before they escalate into larger issues. A seemingly minor disagreement can spiral into a full-blown crisis if left unchecked. Being proactive in addressing small issues will save you time, resources, and relationships in the long run.

Conflict Resolution Strategies

1. Active Listening and Empathy: The cornerstone of any conflict resolution process is active listening. Leaders must demonstrate empathy by fully understanding the perspectives and emotions of each stakeholder. This doesn't mean agreeing with everyone, but rather acknowledging their viewpoints and validating their concerns. Active listening builds trust and creates a foundation upon which solutions can be built.

One practical way to implement active listening is by holding structured meetings where each stakeholder is given equal time to voice their concerns, uninterrupted. The leader's role is to summarize what has been said and ask clarifying questions, ensuring that everyone feels heard before any decisions are made.

2. Interest-Based Negotiation (Getting to the Root Cause): Often, conflicts arise because stakeholders are focused on their positions rather than their underlying interests. A position is what a stakeholder says they want; an interest is why they want it. For instance, a department might demand more budget, but their underlying interest could be improving team performance or meeting customer expectations.

Leaders must guide stakeholders to move beyond positions and identify their true interests. By doing so, it becomes easier to find solutions that satisfy all parties. This approach, known as interest-based negotiation, fosters collaboration rather than competition.

3. Collaborative Problem-Solving: The most effective conflict resolution strategies are collaborative rather than adversarial. When stakeholders work together to solve a problem, they are more likely to arrive at a solution that is sustainable and mutually

beneficial. As a leader, your job is to facilitate this process by creating an environment where collaboration is encouraged and where all stakeholders are engaged in the solution.

Encourage stakeholders to brainstorm together, and emphasize that the goal is not to "win" the argument, but to find the best solution for the organization as a whole. This often involves compromise, but when done correctly, it can lead to a more creative and effective solution than any one stakeholder would have arrived at alone.

4. Mediation and Facilitation: In some cases, conflicts can become so entrenched that the parties involved are unable to resolve them on their own. This is where mediation comes in. A leader, acting as a neutral third party, can help facilitate dialogue between stakeholders, ensuring that the conversation remains focused on solutions rather than blame.

The role of a mediator is not to impose solutions but to guide stakeholders toward their own resolution. This often involves reframing the conflict, helping parties see the issue from a new perspective, and encouraging them to think creatively about potential solutions.

5. Setting Clear Boundaries and Expectations: Conflicts often arise when there is ambiguity around roles, responsibilities, and expectations. By setting clear boundaries and establishing explicit expectations upfront, leaders can prevent many conflicts from arising in the first place.

For example, when managing cross-functional teams, it's important to define the decision-making process clearly. Who has the final say on project deliverables? What criteria will be used to prioritize tasks? By addressing these questions early on, leaders can reduce the likelihood of conflict later.

6. Leveraging Emotional Intelligence (EQ): Emotionally intelligent leaders are better equipped to handle conflicts because they can manage their own emotions and understand the emotions of others. High EQ allows leaders to remain calm under pressure, respond to conflict with empathy rather than defensiveness, and build stronger, more trusting relationships with stakeholders.

Developing EQ involves self-awareness, self-regulation, and social awareness. Leaders should invest time in improving these skills through training and self-reflection, as they are essential for managing the complex emotional dynamics that often accompany conflicts in high-stakes business scenarios.

7. Adapting to Cultural Differences: In an increasingly globalized business environment, leaders must be aware of how cultural differences can influence conflict. What might be seen as direct and assertive communication in one culture could be perceived as confrontational or disrespectful in another. Leaders must develop cultural sensitivity and adapt their conflict resolution strategies accordingly.

For instance, in cultures where face-saving is important, conflicts should be approached in a way that allows all parties to maintain their dignity. This might involve addressing issues privately rather than in a public forum, or framing feedback in a way that emphasizes collective responsibility rather than individual fault.

Balancing Competing Interests: A Strategic Approach

One of the most challenging aspects of conflict resolution is balancing competing interests. Stakeholders often have conflicting priorities, and as a leader, it is your responsibility to ensure that these competing interests are aligned with the organization's broader objectives. This requires a strategic approach that considers both short-term wins and long-term goals.

1. Prioritization and Alignment: Not all interests are equally important. As a leader, you must prioritize interests based on their alignment with the organization's strategic goals. This requires a clear understanding of the company's vision, mission, and values, as well as the ability to communicate these priorities to stakeholders.

2. Creating Win-Win Solutions: Whenever possible, strive to create win-win solutions that meet the needs of all stakeholders. This often involves thinking creatively about how resources can be allocated or how processes can be adjusted to satisfy multiple parties. Leaders must be skilled negotiators, finding common ground where others see only conflict.

3. Compromise with Integrity: In some cases, compromise is necessary. However, it's important to ensure that compromises do not undermine the organization's core values or strategic objectives. Leaders must strike a balance between accommodating stakeholders' needs and maintaining the integrity of the organization's mission.

Turning Conflict into Opportunity

Navigating conflict and managing competing interests is one of the most complex challenges business leaders face. However, with the right strategies, conflict can be transformed from a source of tension into an opportunity for innovation and growth. By fostering open communication, encouraging collaboration, and balancing interests strategically, leaders can build stronger relationships with stakeholders and drive their organizations toward long-term success.

Aligning Stakeholders Towards a Common Goal

In any business, the ability to align stakeholders—whether they are employees, investors, customers, or external partners—towards a common goal is critical for success. However, achieving alignment is easier said than done, particularly when stakeholders have different objectives, interests, or priorities. Without a shared vision, efforts can become fragmented, resources misallocated, and ultimately, the organization's capacity to achieve its strategic objectives will be undermined.

This chapter delves deep into the strategies, principles, and real-world examples of aligning stakeholders towards a unified direction. Through understanding motivations, fostering communication, and setting clear, shared goals, leaders can inspire and guide stakeholders to work together cohesively, maximizing their collective strengths for organizational success.

The Importance of Stakeholder Alignment

Imagine a rowing team where each person rows at a different pace, or even worse, in different directions. Despite everyone's best efforts, the boat will either move very slowly or drift aimlessly in circles. This is analogous to what happens in businesses where stakeholders are not aligned. Without clear alignment, efforts across teams and departments become disjointed, and the organization may fail to achieve its desired outcomes.

Stakeholder alignment ensures that everyone is working toward the same goals with a shared understanding of priorities. When stakeholders are aligned:

- Resources are optimized: Time, energy, and money are invested in initiatives that move the organization forward, not wasted on conflicting interests.

- Collaboration is enhanced: Teams work together rather than in silos, leading to more innovative and effective solutions.

- Accountability increases: When stakeholders share the same vision and goals, there is less finger-pointing and more collective responsibility for outcomes.

The challenge lies in the fact that different stakeholders often have competing interests. Investors may be focused on short-term returns, employees may prioritize job security and a healthy work environment, while customers may demand higher quality products at lower costs. As a leader, it's your job to bring these divergent interests into alignment with the company's overarching strategic objectives.

Key Principles for Aligning Stakeholders

1. Establishing a Clear, Compelling Vision

   The foundation of stakeholder alignment is a well-defined and compelling vision that resonates with all stakeholders. A shared vision acts as a North Star, providing direction and a sense of purpose. It answers the "why" behind the organization's efforts, helping stakeholders understand not just what the goals are, but why those goals matter.

For example, consider the case of Tesla. Tesla's vision is not just about selling electric cars; it's about accelerating the world's transition to sustainable energy. This grand vision resonates with various stakeholders—customers who are environmentally conscious, investors who see the future potential of clean energy, and employees who are motivated by the mission of changing the world. By having a clear and compelling vision, Tesla aligns diverse stakeholders towards a common goal, transcending short-term financial considerations.

To establish a clear vision, leaders must:

- Communicate the vision consistently and clearly across all channels.

- Ensure that the vision connects emotionally with stakeholders, appealing to their values and aspirations.

- Align the vision with the organization's core mission and long-term strategy.

2. Understanding Stakeholder Motivations

Stakeholders are not a homogenous group; each has different needs, concerns, and motivations. Aligning stakeholders requires a deep understanding of what drives them. Investors might be motivated by financial returns, customers by the quality and affordability of products, and employees by opportunities for growth and recognition. The better you understand these motivations, the more effectively you can align them with the organization's goals.

For instance, in a project aimed at implementing new technology within an organization, the IT department might be driven by technical feasibility and innovation, while the finance department may be more concerned about cost control and return on investment. Aligning these stakeholders would require addressing both their concerns—demonstrating how the technology can be implemented within budget while also showcasing the long-term benefits of innovation.

One of the best ways to understand stakeholder motivations is through direct engagement. This could be in the form of one-on-one conversations, focus groups, surveys, or even informal check-ins. The more you engage, the clearer it becomes how to bridge their interests with organizational objectives.

3. Communicating Transparently and Regularly

Effective communication is the glue that holds stakeholder alignment together. In the absence of clear and regular communication, stakeholders may fill in the gaps with their own assumptions, leading to misalignment.

Take, for example, a large-scale merger between two companies. Mergers are notorious for misalignment because employees from both organizations may fear losing their jobs, while shareholders may be unsure how the merger will impact profitability. In such cases, transparent communication is critical. Leaders must consistently communicate the benefits of the merger, address concerns directly, and provide updates throughout the integration process. When stakeholders feel informed and their concerns are acknowledged, they are more likely to align with the company's direction.

Transparent communication is about more than just disseminating information—it's about creating dialogue. Leaders should encourage questions, feedback, and open discussions, ensuring that stakeholders feel heard and included in the process.

4. Creating a Sense of Ownership

Alignment cannot be imposed from the top down. Stakeholders need to feel a sense of ownership over the company's goals. When people feel that they have a stake in the outcome, they are more motivated to work towards the same objectives.

For instance, in organizations that implement employee stock ownership plans (ESOPs), employees are not just workers—they are shareholders. This changes their perspective; they are more invested in the long-term success of the company because their own financial success is tied to it. This sense of ownership aligns employees' personal goals with the company's financial objectives.

Even in situations where equity isn't involved, leaders can create a sense of ownership by involving stakeholders in decision-making processes. For example, before launching a new product, a company might solicit feedback from its customers through beta testing and surveys. By involving customers in the development process, the company fosters a sense of ownership among its user base, making customers feel like partners rather than passive consumers.

5. Aligning Incentives with Goals

Incentives play a crucial role in aligning stakeholders towards a common goal. If incentives are misaligned, stakeholders may pursue their own interests at the expense of the broader organizational goals.

A classic example of misaligned incentives can be found in the 2008 financial crisis, where many executives in the financial industry were rewarded based on short-term profits rather than long-term stability. This led to risky behaviors that ultimately contributed to the collapse of financial institutions. In contrast, companies that structure executive compensation based on long-term performance are more likely to see alignment between management's goals and the long-term health of the organization.

Leaders must carefully design incentives to ensure they promote behaviors that align with the company's goals. This might include performance bonuses tied to team success, customer satisfaction metrics, or long-term financial growth rather than quarterly profits.

6. Building Trust and Accountability

Alignment requires trust—trust that everyone is working towards the same objective, trust that leaders are making decisions in the best interest of the organization, and trust that stakeholders' contributions will be valued and recognized.

Trust is built through consistent actions, transparency, and accountability. Leaders must demonstrate that they are accountable for the success of the team and the organization. When employees see that leadership is willing to take responsibility for both successes and failures, they are more likely to trust the vision and align with the company's goals.

A practical example of building trust can be found in companies like Patagonia, known for its strong commitment to environmental sustainability. By consistently aligning its business practices with its environmental mission, Patagonia has built a high level of trust with both its customers and employees. This trust translates into strong alignment around the company's goals, with employees and customers alike acting as advocates for the brand.

7. Continuous Alignment and Adaptation

Stakeholder alignment is not a one-time event but an ongoing process. As the business environment changes, so too do the interests and priorities of stakeholders. Regularly revisiting the alignment between stakeholders and the organization's goals is crucial to maintaining momentum and avoiding drift.

A real-world example of the need for continuous alignment can be seen in the tech industry, where rapid innovation often leads to shifting priorities. A company like Apple must constantly align its engineering teams, marketing departments, and suppliers around new product launches. As market demands and technologies evolve, Apple regularly reassesses and realigns its stakeholders to ensure continued success. This involves iterative product development cycles, regular feedback loops, and agile project management practices.

Leaders should establish regular checkpoints—whether through quarterly business reviews, stakeholder meetings, or team retrospectives—to reassess alignment and make adjustments where necessary. This continuous realignment ensures that the organization remains agile and responsive to changing conditions.

Real-World Examples of Stakeholder Alignment

1. Starbucks: Aligning Around Corporate Social Responsibility

Starbucks is a prime example of a company that has successfully aligned its stakeholders around a common goal—corporate social responsibility (CSR). From customers to employees and investors, Starbucks has built a brand around sustainability and ethical sourcing. By clearly articulating its commitment to social and environmental issues, Starbucks has aligned its stakeholders around this common goal.

For employees, this alignment comes in the form of benefits like tuition reimbursement and stock options, reinforcing the company's commitment to their personal and professional growth. For customers, Starbucks' alignment with sustainability is evident in its ethical sourcing practices and environmental initiatives, such as the push for recyclable and reusable cups. By aligning stakeholders around a shared commitment to sustainability, Starbucks has strengthened its brand and created a loyal customer base.

2. Google's OKR System: Aligning Teams Through Clear Goals

Google's use of the Objectives and Key Results (OKR) system is a well-known example of how setting clear, measurable goals can align diverse teams and stakeholders towards a common objective. OKRs help Google employees at all levels understand how their work contributes to the company's overall mission. This system creates transparency, accountability, and alignment across the organization.

By setting ambitious yet attainable goals, and then breaking those down into measurable key results, Google ensures that each employee's efforts are aligned with the company's strategic objectives. OKRs are revisited and reassessed regularly, ensuring continuous alignment as the company evolves.

Case Study: Aligning Stakeholders in a Complex Business Environment – The Global Expansion of EcoEnergy

Background of EcoEnergy

EcoEnergy, founded in 2008, had a clear vision from the start: to provide affordable, sustainable energy solutions worldwide. Initially focusing on solar and wind power solutions in North America, the company had grown steadily over the years, gaining a reputation for its commitment to innovation and sustainability.

By 2018, EcoEnergy faced a critical juncture—its leadership team wanted to expand into emerging markets in Asia and Africa. These regions presented both vast opportunities and significant challenges, including varying government regulations, cultural differences, infrastructure gaps, and financial risks.

Let's discuss how EcoEnergy aligned its key stakeholders—investors, employees, local governments, and partners—around this ambitious expansion plan.

STEP 1: CRAFTING A CLEAR, COMPELLING VISION FOR GLOBAL EXPANSION

At the heart of EcoEnergy's success was its ability to craft a compelling vision that united its stakeholders. The company didn't just frame this expansion as a new business opportunity; instead, they positioned it as a mission-driven initiative to provide sustainable energy access to under-served populations, improving lives and helping combat climate change on a global scale.

Audience Question:

Why do you think it was important for EcoEnergy to frame their expansion as a mission-driven initiative rather than just a business opportunity?

> Answer:

Framing the expansion as a mission-driven initiative allowed EcoEnergy to tap into the deeper motivations of its stakeholders. Investors were drawn to the long-term value associated with socially responsible investments. Employees felt they were part of a purpose greater than profit, inspiring a stronger commitment. Local governments and international partners also aligned with the sustainability goals, making negotiations smoother.

The vision clearly articulated how the global expansion aligned with the core mission of the company and the values of its stakeholders, creating an emotional and ethical connection beyond mere financial growth.

STEP 2: UNDERSTANDING AND ADDRESSING STAKEHOLDER MOTIVATIONS

To gain the support of diverse stakeholders, EcoEnergy first needed to understand their unique motivations. Let's look at the different groups involved:

- Investors: For them, profitability was paramount, but they were also increasingly interested in the environmental and social impacts of their investments.

- Employees: The engineering and operations teams were excited about the technical challenges, but they also wanted assurance that their work conditions would be safe and that the company would maintain ethical labor practices in foreign markets.

- Local Governments in Emerging Markets: Their focus was on creating jobs, boosting their economies, and ensuring affordable energy solutions for their populations.

- Partners and Suppliers: They sought reliable contracts, clear communication, and alignment with their own corporate responsibility goals.

EcoEnergy's leadership spent significant time engaging with each stakeholder group to understand their specific concerns and expectations.

Audience Engagement:

What are some ways EcoEnergy's leadership could have engaged with these stakeholders to gain a deeper understanding of their motivations?

> Answer:

EcoEnergy employed several strategies to gather input from its stakeholders:

- Investors were engaged through regular town halls and one-on-one meetings to discuss the long-term financial returns of the expansion.

- Employees were surveyed and included in feedback sessions to address their concerns about safety and working conditions in new markets.

- Local governments were involved through diplomatic meetings and economic impact studies, showing the potential benefits of increased energy access and job creation.

- Partners and suppliers were invited to strategic planning sessions where they could voice their expectations for ethical sourcing and reliable payment terms.

By understanding and addressing these motivations, EcoEnergy tailored its global expansion strategy to meet the needs of its stakeholders, aligning them towards a shared goal.

STEP 3: TRANSPARENT AND REGULAR COMMUNICATION

One of the biggest risks EcoEnergy faced was losing stakeholder support if communication became unclear or inconsistent. To counter this, the company developed a communication strategy focused on transparency, frequency, and openness to feedback.

They set up multiple communication channels, including:

- Monthly investor updates highlighting progress, risks, and opportunities.

- Internal newsletters and all-hands meetings for employees, where leadership shared updates and recognized individual contributions to the global expansion.

- Public press releases and media engagements with local governments to demonstrate the positive impact EcoEnergy was bringing to emerging markets.

When unexpected challenges arose—such as delays in securing permits in certain regions—EcoEnergy openly communicated the setbacks, along with their strategies to overcome them. This openness prevented stakeholders from becoming disillusioned or disengaged.

Audience Engagement:

Why do you think EcoEnergy's transparency during challenges was key to maintaining stakeholder alignment?

> Answer:

Being transparent during challenges showed that EcoEnergy was committed to being honest and accountable, even when things didn't go according to plan. This built trust among stakeholders, who felt they were informed partners in the process rather than being kept in the dark. Investors appreciated the honesty, employees felt respected, and local governments saw EcoEnergy as a reliable and responsible business partner.

STEP 4: ALIGNING INCENTIVES AND BUILDING A SENSE OF OWNERSHIP

Another important step EcoEnergy took was aligning incentives across all stakeholders. They introduced a shared success model, where each group stood to gain from the expansion's success:

- Investors were offered long-term value incentives, with bonus payouts tied not only to financial milestones but also to social impact goals, such as the number of new homes powered by sustainable energy.

- Employees were given stock options, aligning their personal financial success with the company's global success. Additionally, EcoEnergy developed recognition programs for those who contributed to problem-solving in the new markets.

- Local governments were offered partnership agreements that guaranteed the creation of jobs and infrastructure investment, ensuring mutual benefits from the expansion.

EcoEnergy also involved stakeholders in decision-making processes where possible. For example, before finalizing the expansion strategy, the company invited its top engineers and regional experts to co-create solutions for the specific challenges in Asia and Africa. By giving them a voice in shaping the plan, EcoEnergy created a deeper sense of ownership over the outcome.

Audience Engagement:

What impact do you think involving stakeholders in decision-making had on the alignment process?

> Answer:

Involving stakeholders in decision-making helped foster a sense of ownership and accountability. When stakeholders feel they have contributed to shaping a strategy or plan, they are more likely to support it wholeheartedly. Employees, for instance, felt a personal connection to the project's success, knowing their ideas had been considered. For local governments, this approach strengthened diplomatic relations and trust, ensuring that their interests were fully integrated into the plan.

Outcome and Lessons Learned

By 2021, EcoEnergy had successfully entered three major emerging markets—India, Kenya, and the Philippines. The company's focus on aligning its stakeholders paid off in numerous ways:

- Investors saw strong returns as the company expanded its market presence and met both financial and social impact goals.

- Employees were highly engaged, with retention rates improving due to the shared sense of purpose and the financial incentives aligned with the company's success.

- Local governments publicly praised EcoEnergy's commitment to creating jobs and providing affordable, sustainable energy to their citizens.

- Partners found long-term contracts with EcoEnergy reliable and rewarding, fostering ongoing collaboration.

Audience Reflection:

Reflecting on EcoEnergy's journey, let's consider how your own organizations could benefit from stakeholder alignment.

- Do you have a clear and compelling vision that resonates with your stakeholders?

- Are you regularly engaging with them to understand their motivations and concerns?

- How transparent is your communication, particularly during times of challenge?

- Are your stakeholders given opportunities to contribute to decision-making, and do they feel a sense of ownership?

EcoEnergy's success underscores the critical importance of aligning stakeholders around a common goal. By building trust, fostering open communication, and creating incentives that align with stakeholder interests, the company navigated the complexities of global expansion while maintaining the support of its key players. Their journey is a testament to the power of alignment in achieving long-term, sustainable success.

Let's take these lessons forward and apply them to our own stakeholder relationships.

CHAPTER 5: THE LONG GAME: BALANCING SHORT-TERM GAINS WITH LONG-TERM VISION

In today's fast-paced business landscape, it is easy to become consumed by the pursuit of immediate results. The pressure to deliver quarterly earnings, hit sales targets, or respond to market fluctuations can be overwhelming. Businesses, especially those in competitive sectors, often find themselves fixated on short-term gains—decisions that yield quick rewards but may come at the expense of future growth. However, the truly successful enterprises are those that strike a delicate balance between short-term wins and long-term vision, keeping their sights set on sustainable growth while navigating the present-day challenges.

At the heart of this balance lies a strategic mindset that prioritizes not just immediate profitability but also long-term impact, innovation, and the company's broader purpose. Leaders who master the art of the long game understand that while short-term gains can create momentum, they must be aligned with a larger, more enduring vision. They make decisions not just for the next quarter, but for the next decade, and beyond. This chapter delves into the complexities of balancing these seemingly opposing forces—short-term profitability and long-term sustainability—and how to maintain focus on the bigger picture without sacrificing immediate results.

The Temptation of Short-Termism

The allure of short-term success is difficult to resist. Financial markets, shareholders, and even internal stakeholders often demand immediate performance indicators, creating an environment where short-termism dominates. In this context, it is easy for companies to prioritize decisions that maximize immediate revenue or minimize costs in the short run—slashing research and development (R&D) budgets, downsizing staff, or cutting back on marketing. While these actions may satisfy short-term financial goals, they can severely undermine a company's ability to innovate and remain competitive in the long term.

The consequences of short-termism are not merely hypothetical. History is rife with examples of companies that prioritized short-term gains at the expense of long-term viability. Take the example of Kodak, a dominant player in the photography industry. The company was well-positioned to lead the digital photography revolution but was too focused on protecting its film business—a short-term priority. By the time Kodak tried to pivot, it was too late, and it filed for bankruptcy. The lesson here is stark: without a focus on long-term strategy, even market leaders can become obsolete.

On the other hand, companies like Amazon, which has consistently reinvested profits into new ventures and long-term projects, have shown that short-term sacrifices can pay off handsomely in the long run. Amazon famously did not turn a profit for its first several years, but its founder, Jeff Bezos, remained committed to a long-term vision of building the "Everything Store." This long-term focus, even in the face of criticism, allowed Amazon to develop its infrastructure, dominate e-commerce, and later expand into cloud computing, streaming services, and AI technologies. Today, it is one of the most valuable companies in the world, precisely because it balanced short-term operational needs with long-term strategic goals.

The Long-Term Vision: Building a Future-Proof Business

To play the long game effectively, leaders must first have a clear long-term vision. This vision is the North Star that guides decision-making, ensuring that short-term actions are always aligned with broader, more enduring goals. A long-term vision allows companies to remain agile and innovative while still being grounded in a stable strategic framework.

Crafting this vision is not a simple task. It requires deep reflection on where the company wants to be in five, ten, or even twenty years. More importantly, it involves understanding the broader forces that will shape the industry and society in the future—technological advancements, demographic shifts, changing consumer behaviors, and environmental challenges. A long-term vision must be adaptable, yet firm enough to serve as a guidepost for decision-making. It should inspire employees, attract customers, and reassure investors that the company is not merely chasing the latest trend but is thoughtfully building for the future.

A powerful example of long-term vision is Tesla, whose CEO, Elon Musk, has been unrelenting in his goal of advancing sustainable energy. Musk's vision of a future where electric vehicles (EVs) dominate the roads and solar energy powers homes has shaped Tesla's strategy from day one. Even in the face of initial skepticism, production delays, and financial losses, Tesla has stayed the course, continually investing in innovation, battery technology, and infrastructure. Today, Tesla is not only a leader in the EV market but is also reshaping industries well beyond the automotive sector, proving that a compelling long-term vision can turn even the most audacious goals into reality.

Balancing Short-Term and Long-Term Strategies

While a long-term vision is critical, it is equally important to manage short-term pressures. After all, businesses need to remain profitable in the present to fund their future ambitions. The key to balancing short-term and long-term strategies lies in prioritization and alignment.

First, companies need to identify which short-term actions will serve as stepping stones toward long-term goals. This requires a clear understanding of how immediate operational decisions—whether related to hiring, marketing, or product development—fit into the broader picture. For instance, a company might choose to invest in short-term customer acquisition strategies, not just to boost immediate revenue but to build a loyal customer base that will drive future growth. Similarly, a company may delay immediate profitability in favor of investing in technology or infrastructure that will provide a competitive edge in the future.

Second, businesses need to establish key performance indicators (KPIs) that reflect both short-term achievements and long-term progress. While quarterly earnings are important, companies should also measure indicators such as customer satisfaction, employee retention, and innovation capacity. These metrics provide a more holistic view of the company's health and its readiness to thrive in the future.

Take the example of Apple, a company known for its ability to balance short-term profitability with long-term innovation. Apple's decision to invest heavily in R&D and design, even when it was not immediately profitable, allowed it to build iconic products like the iPhone, which revolutionized the technology industry. Apple did not sacrifice long-term innovation for short-term gains; instead, it found a way to continuously innovate while maintaining its financial performance. This approach has enabled Apple to remain at the forefront of consumer technology for decades.

The Role of Leadership in Playing the Long Game

Leadership plays a crucial role in maintaining focus on the long game. It is the responsibility of leaders to not only craft a compelling long-term vision but also to communicate it effectively to all stakeholders—employees, customers, and investors alike. When leaders articulate a clear vision, they create a sense of purpose that can inspire and motivate teams, even in the face of short-term challenges.

One of the greatest challenges for leaders is managing stakeholder expectations, particularly when short-term results fall short of projections. In such moments, it is critical for leaders to reinforce the importance of long-term goals and to explain how current setbacks are part of the journey toward a larger objective. Leaders must also be willing to make tough decisions, such as sacrificing short-term gains for long-term value creation.

Consider the case of Microsoft's Satya Nadella, who transformed the company by shifting its focus from traditional software products to cloud computing. Under Nadella's leadership, Microsoft pivoted away from short-term revenue models, such as software licensing, to invest in its Azure cloud platform. This was a bold move that required patience and a strong long-term vision, but today, Azure is one of Microsoft's most profitable divisions, helping the company to maintain its leadership in the tech industry.

Staying Agile in a Long-Term Strategy

One of the misconceptions about long-term strategies is that they are rigid and unchanging. In reality, the most successful long-term strategies are those that allow for agility and flexibility. The business environment is constantly evolving, and companies must be able to pivot when necessary without losing sight of their overarching goals.

Agility does not mean abandoning a long-term vision; rather, it means being adaptable in the tactics and strategies used to achieve that vision. For example, a company may need to shift its product development focus based on changing customer needs or technological advancements, but the overall goal of delivering innovative solutions remains the same. The ability to adapt quickly to new information while staying committed to the larger picture is a hallmark of companies that successfully balance short-term and long-term strategies.

An excellent example of agility within a long-term framework is Netflix. The company started as a DVD rental service, but its long-term vision was always to be at the forefront of home entertainment. As streaming technology became viable, Netflix quickly pivoted to a subscription-based streaming model, recognizing the shift in consumer behavior. This move required short-term investments that initially reduced profitability, but it was a critical step in achieving its long-term goal of becoming a global entertainment leader.

Fostering a Culture of Long-Term Thinking

Finally, for companies to successfully play the long game, they must foster a culture that values long-term thinking. This begins with hiring and developing talent that understands the importance of both immediate performance and future growth. It also involves creating an environment where employees are encouraged to think creatively about the future, take calculated risks, and innovate without fear of short-term setbacks.

A culture of long-term thinking is nurtured when leaders reward employees not just for meeting short-term targets, but also for contributing to the company's long-term success. This might include recognizing those who propose innovative ideas, lead strategic initiatives, or demonstrate a commitment to the company's broader mission. By aligning rewards and incentives with long-term goals, companies can build a workforce that is invested in the company's future, not just its present.

Playing the long game is not about choosing between short-term and long-term success— it's about mastering the delicate balance between the two. Companies that succeed in this regard understand that while short-term gains are necessary to fuel day-to-day operations, they must always be in service of a larger, more strategic vision. By maintaining focus on the bigger picture, investing in innovation, and fostering a culture of long-term thinking, organizations can position themselves not only to survive but to thrive in a constantly evolving business landscape.

Strategic Investments for Future Success

A crucial aspect of maintaining a long-term focus is making strategic investments that align with the company's vision. These investments can take many forms, including technology upgrades, workforce development, and expansion into new markets. While such initiatives often require significant upfront costs and may not yield immediate financial returns, they are essential for building a resilient organization that can adapt to future challenges and opportunities.

For example, companies in the technology sector are frequently faced with rapid changes in consumer preferences and advancements in technology. By investing in R&D, businesses can stay ahead of the curve, developing innovative products and services that anticipate market needs. This forward-thinking approach not only enhances competitive advantage but also establishes the company as a leader in its industry. When organizations consistently invest in innovation and improvement, they cultivate a reputation for excellence that attracts top talent, loyal customers, and investor confidence.

Moreover, investing in employee development is a powerful way to secure long-term success. Organizations that prioritize continuous learning and skill development create a more agile and adaptable workforce. This, in turn, enables them to respond to new challenges and seize emerging opportunities more effectively. Programs that encourage upskilling, cross-training, and leadership development not only benefit individual employees but also foster a culture of growth and resilience within the organization.

Building Strategic Partnerships

In addition to internal investments, forming strategic partnerships can be a vital component of a long-term strategy. Collaborating with other organizations, whether through joint ventures, alliances, or partnerships, can open doors to new markets, technologies, and customer segments. These partnerships can be particularly beneficial when entering unfamiliar territories or navigating complex regulatory environments.

For instance, the collaboration between tech giants like Microsoft and companies such as LinkedIn demonstrates the power of strategic partnerships. Microsoft's acquisition of LinkedIn not only expanded its reach into the social media space but also integrated valuable data and networking capabilities into its suite of business solutions. This partnership allowed Microsoft to enhance its offerings while maintaining a long-term vision of becoming the go-to platform for business productivity and professional networking.

Forming alliances with startups can foster innovation by providing access to cutting-edge technologies and fresh perspectives. Companies can leverage the agility and creativity of smaller firms to drive innovation while benefiting from the stability and resources of larger organizations. This synergy can create a dynamic environment where both parties can thrive, ultimately leading to long-term success.

Navigating Uncertainty with a Long-Term Perspective

In an era defined by rapid change and unpredictability, organizations must also be adept at navigating uncertainty. Economic fluctuations, global crises, and shifting market dynamics can all disrupt even the most well-laid plans. However, a long-term perspective equips leaders with the resilience needed to adapt to such challenges without losing sight of their core mission.

For instance, during the COVID-19 pandemic, many companies faced unprecedented challenges that tested their business models and operations. Those with a strong long-term vision were able to pivot quickly, reimagining their strategies to accommodate changing consumer behaviors and preferences. Companies that prioritized digital transformation, for example, were better positioned to thrive in a remote environment. They adapted their operations, enhancing online services and improving digital customer experiences, all while staying true to their long-term objectives.

In addition, organizations that embrace a culture of experimentation are better equipped to navigate uncertainty. By encouraging employees to take risks, test new ideas, and learn from failures, companies can foster innovation and agility. This iterative approach allows organizations to respond to changing circumstances with creativity and confidence, ultimately reinforcing their long-term vision.

Communicating the Long Game

Effective communication is a fundamental component of maintaining focus on the long game. Leaders must consistently articulate the company's vision and strategy to all stakeholders, ensuring that everyone understands the rationale behind key decisions. Clear communication not only fosters alignment but also builds trust among employees, customers, and investors.

To achieve this, leaders should share both short-term and long-term goals transparently, illustrating how immediate actions contribute to the broader vision. Regular updates and progress reports can help keep stakeholders informed and engaged, reinforcing a sense of shared purpose. Moreover, leveraging storytelling as a tool for communication can make the company's journey more relatable and inspiring, creating a narrative that resonates with audiences on an emotional level.

Additionally, seeking feedback from employees and stakeholders can strengthen commitment to the long game. Engaging in open dialogue about the company's vision allows leaders to address concerns, clarify misunderstandings, and foster a sense of ownership among team members. When employees feel invested in the company's long-term success, they are more likely to contribute their best efforts and support the organization's strategic direction.

A Roadmap for Sustainable Success

Balancing short-term gains with a long-term vision is a critical challenge that all businesses must navigate. The ability to prioritize immediate needs while remaining focused on broader objectives is essential for achieving sustainable success in today's dynamic environment. Leaders who embrace the long game understand that immediate results should not come at the cost of future viability; instead, they recognize that the two can coexist harmoniously.

By cultivating a clear long-term vision, making strategic investments, fostering a culture of innovation, and communicating effectively, organizations can create a roadmap for lasting success. As businesses continue to face a myriad of challenges, those that commit to balancing short-term and long-term priorities will not only survive but thrive. The journey may be complex, but with a strategic mindset and a steadfast commitment to the future, organizations can position themselves as leaders in their industries, ready to seize the opportunities that lie ahead.

The long game is not just a strategy; it is a mindset—a commitment to building a future that transcends immediate results. By maintaining focus on the bigger picture, businesses can navigate high-stakes scenarios with confidence, ensuring that today's decisions contribute to tomorrow's success. As we move forward in an increasingly uncertain world, let us embrace the long game and strive for sustainable growth that empowers both organizations and the communities they serve.

Ensuring Sustainable Growth Amidst Uncertainty

In today's rapidly changing business environment, organizations face unprecedented challenges that require a keen understanding of the interplay between uncertainty and sustainable growth. Economic fluctuations, technological disruptions, and shifting consumer preferences create a landscape where businesses must not only adapt but also thrive. Sustainable growth is not merely about achieving financial success; it encompasses environmental stewardship, social responsibility, and long-term strategic vision. This chapter delves into the various strategies that organizations can employ to ensure sustainable growth amidst uncertainty, supported by real-world examples and practical insights.

Understanding the Landscape of Uncertainty

To navigate uncertainty effectively, organizations must first understand its multifaceted nature. Uncertainty can arise from various sources, including economic downturns, geopolitical tensions, technological advancements, and environmental changes. Each of these factors can disrupt traditional business models and necessitate a reevaluation of strategies.

For instance, the COVID-19 pandemic exemplified how quickly uncertainty can alter the business landscape. Companies across sectors faced sudden closures, supply chain disruptions, and shifts in consumer behavior. Those that were able to pivot quickly and embrace new business models found opportunities for growth amidst chaos. For example, restaurants that had primarily relied on dine-in customers swiftly adapted by enhancing their delivery services, creating meal kits, or offering outdoor dining experiences. This adaptability not only helped them survive the immediate crisis but also positioned them for future growth by diversifying their revenue streams.

Cultivating an Agile Mindset

One of the key components of ensuring sustainable growth in uncertain times is cultivating an agile mindset within the organization. Agility allows businesses to respond quickly to changing circumstances and seize opportunities as they arise. This involves fostering a culture of flexibility, continuous learning, and experimentation.

A compelling example of agility in action can be seen in the retail sector, particularly with companies like Zara. By implementing a fast fashion model, Zara has successfully maintained a responsive supply chain that allows it to introduce new collections based on current trends within weeks. This approach not only meets consumer demands promptly but also minimizes excess inventory, reducing waste and enhancing sustainability. Zara's ability to adapt to market trends while ensuring ethical sourcing and production practices exemplifies how agility can drive sustainable growth.

Businesses can cultivate agility by embracing technology and data analytics. Companies that leverage real-time data to monitor market trends and customer preferences can make informed decisions quickly. For example, Netflix utilizes advanced algorithms to analyze viewer behavior and preferences, enabling it to tailor its content offerings. By understanding what its audience desires, Netflix can pivot its programming strategy swiftly, ensuring continued subscriber growth and engagement.

Building Resilience Through Diversification

Diversification is another critical strategy for ensuring sustainable growth amidst uncertainty. By expanding product lines, services, or market reach, organizations can mitigate risks associated with over-reliance on a single revenue stream. This approach enhances resilience and allows businesses to weather fluctuations in demand or market conditions.

A notable example of diversification is Amazon. Originally an online bookstore, Amazon has successfully expanded its offerings to include everything from cloud computing services (Amazon Web Services) to streaming services (Amazon Prime Video). This diversification not only increases revenue streams but also positions Amazon as a key player in various industries, reducing its vulnerability to economic downturns in any single sector. The company's strategic investments in logistics, technology, and customer experience further reinforce its resilience and ability to adapt to changing market dynamics.

Additionally, businesses can diversify their supply chains to minimize risk. Companies like Apple have learned the importance of having multiple suppliers for critical components to avoid disruptions. By diversifying its supply chain and establishing relationships with suppliers in different geographic regions, Apple can mitigate risks associated with geopolitical tensions or natural disasters. This strategic approach not only ensures continuity in production but also enhances the company's overall sustainability.

Emphasizing Environmental and Social Responsibility

In the pursuit of sustainable growth, organizations must also prioritize environmental and social responsibility. Consumers are increasingly making purchasing decisions based on a company's commitment to sustainability and ethical practices. Therefore, integrating environmental, social, and governance (ESG) factors into business strategies is essential for long-term success.

Companies like Unilever have demonstrated that sustainable practices can lead to both growth and positive societal impact. Unilever's Sustainable Living Plan focuses on reducing the company's environmental footprint while enhancing the well-being of communities. By committing to sustainable sourcing, reducing plastic waste, and promoting gender equality, Unilever has not only strengthened its brand reputation but also attracted socially conscious consumers. This alignment of business goals with societal values has translated into sustained growth, even in a competitive market.

Another example is Tesla, which has revolutionized the automotive industry by prioritizing sustainability. Tesla's commitment to producing electric vehicles (EVs) aligns with the growing demand for eco-friendly transportation. By focusing on innovation and sustainable practices, Tesla has positioned itself as a leader in the EV market, experiencing substantial growth as consumers shift away from traditional combustion engine vehicles.

Investing in Innovation and Technology

Innovation is a critical driver of sustainable growth in uncertain times. Organizations that prioritize research and development (R&D) can stay ahead of market trends and technological advancements. Investing in innovation allows businesses to create new products, improve existing offerings, and enhance operational efficiency.

Consider the pharmaceutical industry, which has historically faced significant challenges related to regulatory changes and market competition. Companies like Pfizer have demonstrated the importance of innovation in navigating uncertainty. The rapid development of the COVID-19 vaccine showcased Pfizer's ability to leverage its extensive R&D capabilities and collaborate with partners like BioNTech. This swift response not only addressed an urgent global health crisis but also reinforced Pfizer's reputation as a leader in pharmaceutical innovation, driving long-term growth opportunities.

Organizations can embrace digital transformation to enhance their innovation capabilities. Companies that invest in advanced technologies such as artificial intelligence (AI), machine learning, and automation can streamline processes and enhance decision-making. For example, the retail giant Walmart has embraced AI and data analytics to optimize its supply chain and improve inventory management. By leveraging technology to enhance operational efficiency, Walmart has ensured sustainable growth while remaining responsive to consumer demands.

Fostering Collaboration and Partnerships

Collaboration and partnerships play a crucial role in ensuring sustainable growth amidst uncertainty. By leveraging the strengths of other organizations, businesses can enhance their capabilities, access new markets, and share risks. Collaborative approaches can lead to innovative solutions and create synergies that drive growth.

One notable example of collaboration is the partnership between Starbucks and Nestlé. This strategic alliance allows Starbucks to leverage Nestlé's extensive distribution network to expand its coffee products globally. By combining their expertise, the two companies have increased their market reach while sharing resources and reducing the risks associated with entering new markets. This collaboration illustrates how partnerships can facilitate sustainable growth in an uncertain landscape.

Businesses can benefit from engaging with startups and emerging companies. By collaborating with innovative startups, established organizations can tap into new ideas and technologies. For instance, companies like Johnson & Johnson have established innovation hubs that partner with startups in the healthcare sector. This collaborative approach enables Johnson & Johnson to stay at the forefront of medical advancements while supporting the growth of emerging entrepreneurs.

Creating a Culture of Sustainability

Sustainable growth is not solely the responsibility of leadership; it requires a collective effort throughout the organization. Creating a culture of sustainability empowers employees to contribute to the company's long-term vision. When employees are engaged and aligned with the organization's values, they become advocates for sustainable practices and innovation.

Organizations can foster a culture of sustainability by providing training and resources that empower employees to make informed decisions. For example, companies like Patagonia have established initiatives that encourage employees to participate in environmental advocacy and community engagement. By involving employees in sustainability efforts,

Patagonia has not only enhanced its brand reputation but also cultivated a loyal customer base that shares its values.

Additionally, companies can implement incentive programs that reward employees for innovative ideas and sustainable practices. For instance, Unilever has established internal innovation competitions that encourage employees to propose projects that align with the company's sustainability goals. By incentivizing creativity and collaboration, organizations can tap into the collective intelligence of their workforce and drive sustainable growth.

Measuring and Reporting Progress

To ensure sustainable growth amidst uncertainty, organizations must establish metrics and reporting frameworks to assess their progress. By measuring key performance indicators (KPIs) related to sustainability, businesses can identify areas for improvement and demonstrate accountability to stakeholders.

Many companies have adopted sustainability reporting frameworks, such as the Global Reporting Initiative (GRI) and the Sustainability Accounting Standards Board (SASB). These frameworks provide guidance on measuring and disclosing environmental and social performance. For example, companies like Coca-Cola have embraced sustainability reporting to communicate their progress toward reducing water usage and increasing recycling rates. By transparently sharing their efforts, Coca-Cola enhances its reputation and builds trust among consumers and investors.

Organizations can utilize technology to monitor and analyze sustainability metrics in real-time. By leveraging data analytics and reporting tools, businesses can gain insights into their performance and make informed decisions. For instance, General Electric (GE) has implemented a digital platform that allows it to track and report on sustainability initiatives across its operations. This data-driven approach enables GE to identify trends, measure impact, and refine its strategies for sustainable growth.

Navigating the Future with Confidence

In conclusion, ensuring sustainable growth amidst uncertainty requires a multifaceted approach that encompasses agility, diversification, innovation, collaboration, and a commitment to environmental and social responsibility. As organizations navigate an increasingly complex landscape, those that prioritize sustainability will be better positioned to thrive in the face of challenges.

By cultivating an agile mindset, investing in innovation, and fostering collaboration, businesses can create a resilient foundation for growth. Moreover, integrating sustainability into core business practices not only enhances brand reputation but also meets the evolving expectations of consumers and stakeholders.

As we move forward, organizations must embrace the opportunities presented by uncertainty while remaining steadfast in their commitment to sustainable growth. The journey may be challenging, but by leveraging the lessons learned from real-world examples and implementing practical strategies, businesses can navigate the future with confidence and purpose. Ultimately, sustainable growth is not just a goal; it is a commitment to building a better, more resilient world for future generations.

APPENDICES

Appendix A: Decision-Making Models and Tools

In the high-stakes world of business, effective decision-making is not just a skill—it's an imperative. Leaders face complex, multifaceted challenges where a single wrong move can have far-reaching consequences. In this context, structured decision-making models and tools are invaluable. They provide frameworks that help cut through ambiguity, allowing leaders to assess situations systematically, explore alternatives, and select the most advantageous course of action. This appendix aims to provide a comprehensive overview of key decision-making models and tools that have been tried and tested in various business environments, ensuring they are practical, strategic, and action-oriented.

1. The Rational Decision-Making Model

The Rational Decision-Making Model is one of the most well-known and widely used frameworks in business. It is a step-by-step approach designed to make logical, objective decisions based on a systematic analysis of information.

The model typically follows six core steps:

- Problem Identification: The first step involves clearly defining the problem or opportunity. In a business context, this may mean identifying a gap in the market, a drop in performance, or an operational inefficiency.

- Information Gathering: Once the problem is identified, decision-makers collect relevant data. This data might come from internal metrics, market research, competitor analysis, or financial reports.

- Evaluation of Alternatives: At this stage, leaders brainstorm potential solutions or actions. It's critical to consider all possible options, even those that may seem less conventional, as they might offer unexpected benefits.

- Weighing the Evidence: Each alternative is evaluated based on criteria such as cost, feasibility, impact on stakeholders, and alignment with long-term strategic goals.

- Choosing the Best Alternative: After weighing the pros and cons, leaders select the option that offers the greatest benefit with the least risk.

- Implementation and Monitoring: Finally, the decision is implemented, and progress is monitored. Feedback loops are essential here to ensure the decision is producing the desired outcome, and adjustments can be made as needed.

Though logical and structured, the Rational Decision-Making Model can sometimes be limited by real-world constraints, such as time pressure or incomplete information. Nevertheless, it remains a robust tool, particularly in scenarios where sufficient data is available, and decisions can be made without urgency.

2. SWOT Analysis (Strengths, Weaknesses, Opportunities, Threats)

SWOT analysis is a versatile and widely applied tool in decision-making, especially when leaders need to take a comprehensive view of their current situation. This model helps to create a snapshot of both internal and external factors that could influence decision outcomes.

- Strengths: What are the organization's competitive advantages? What unique assets, capabilities, or resources can be leveraged?

- Weaknesses: What internal limitations exist that could hinder performance? These could include gaps in skills, technology, or organizational culture.

- Opportunities: What external factors provide potential growth or advancement opportunities? These might include emerging markets, technological advancements, or changes in customer behavior.

- Threats: What external risks could negatively impact the organization? Economic downturns, regulatory changes, and increased competition are examples of potential threats.

SWOT analysis is particularly useful in strategic planning, allowing leaders to align their decisions with both internal competencies and external market dynamics. However, while SWOT provides a broad view, it should be complemented with other tools that offer more in-depth insights into specific areas.

3. The Pareto Principle (80/20 Rule)

The Pareto Principle, or the 80/20 Rule, is an essential tool for decision-makers in fast-paced business environments where time and resources are limited. The principle suggests that 80% of outcomes result from 20% of causes, and the goal of this tool is to help focus efforts on the most impactful factors.

In practice, this means identifying the key drivers that will yield the most significant results, whether in sales, customer satisfaction, or operational efficiency. For example, a company may find that 80% of its profits come from 20% of its products or customers. By focusing attention on this critical 20%, organizations can optimize their efforts and maximize returns.

The 80/20 Rule is particularly valuable when leaders are confronted with multiple tasks, allowing them to prioritize effectively. However, it is not a precise mathematical rule, and should be applied as a guiding principle rather than a rigid law. Decision-makers must still use judgment in identifying the most critical factors in any situation.

4. Decision Trees

A decision tree is a graphical representation of possible decisions and their associated outcomes. This tool is highly effective for visualizing complex scenarios where multiple paths and potential outcomes need to be considered. Each branch of the tree represents a decision or action, with further branches indicating the possible outcomes of that decision.

The advantage of using decision trees lies in their ability to map out a wide range of options and associated risks. They are particularly helpful in situations that involve uncertainty or where probabilities need to be factored into the decision-making process.

For example, a company considering a major investment in a new product might use a decision tree to evaluate various market scenarios, competitor reactions, and consumer responses. By assigning probabilities to different outcomes and calculating the expected value of each decision path, leaders can make more informed and strategic choices.

Decision trees are particularly useful in project management, risk assessment, and strategic planning. However, they can become complex when dealing with a large number of variables, and decision-makers must be careful not to overcomplicate the model.

5. Cost-Benefit Analysis (CBA)

Cost-Benefit Analysis is a simple yet powerful tool for evaluating decisions based on their potential costs and benefits. This model involves identifying and quantifying all costs associated with a decision—both direct and indirect—and comparing them with the expected benefits.

Costs may include financial investments, time, human resources, and potential risks, while benefits could encompass revenue growth, efficiency improvements, or strategic advantages. By assigning a monetary value to each factor, leaders can calculate whether the benefits outweigh the costs, making it easier to justify their decisions.

CBA is particularly useful in budgeting, resource allocation, and investment decisions. It is also valuable for assessing the long-term impact of strategic initiatives. However, one limitation of CBA is that not all factors can be easily quantified—intangible benefits, such as employee morale or brand reputation, may be difficult to assess in financial terms.

6. The Delphi Technique

The Delphi Technique is a method used for gathering insights and opinions from a group of experts to inform decision-making. This technique is particularly effective in situations where decisions involve uncertainty or complex variables, such as forecasting future trends, assessing risks, or developing innovative solutions.

The process involves a series of structured questionnaires or surveys that are sent to experts, whose responses are anonymized to prevent bias. After each round of feedback, the results are summarized and shared with the group, allowing participants to refine their responses based on the collective input.

The Delphi Technique helps to avoid the dominance of a single opinion or groupthink, ensuring that decisions are informed by a wide range of perspectives. It is especially useful in long-term planning, innovation strategy, and risk management.

However, this method can be time-consuming, as it requires multiple rounds of input. It may also be less effective if the experts involved do not have deep knowledge or if there is insufficient diversity of opinion in the group.

7. Scenario Planning

Scenario planning is a forward-looking tool that helps decision-makers anticipate possible futures and develop strategies to navigate them. This approach is particularly useful in highly volatile or uncertain environments, such as markets undergoing rapid technological change, regulatory shifts, or economic disruption.

The process begins by identifying key uncertainties and trends that could shape the future, such as technological breakthroughs, changes in consumer behavior, or geopolitical risks. Decision-makers then develop a series of plausible scenarios, each representing a different potential future. For each scenario, leaders create strategies that would be effective under those specific conditions.

The value of scenario planning lies in its ability to prepare organizations for a range of possible outcomes, reducing the likelihood of being blindsided by unexpected events. It encourages flexible thinking and adaptive strategies, making businesses more resilient in the face of uncertainty.

Scenario planning is commonly used in strategic planning, risk management, and innovation strategy. However, the success of this tool depends on the quality of the assumptions used to build the scenarios. Over-reliance on a single scenario or failure to update assumptions as conditions change can reduce the effectiveness of the model.

8. The Six Thinking Hats

Developed by Edward de Bono, the Six Thinking Hats model is a tool that encourages decision-makers to look at problems from multiple perspectives. Each "hat" represents a different mode of thinking, helping teams to break out of habitual thought patterns and consider alternative approaches.

- White Hat: Focuses on facts, data, and objective information.

- Red Hat: Considers emotions, feelings, and intuition.

- Black Hat: Identifies risks, challenges, and potential problems.

- Yellow Hat: Looks for positive aspects, opportunities, and potential benefits.

- Green Hat: Encourages creativity, innovation, and new ideas.

- Blue Hat: Focuses on process management, guiding the overall flow of thinking.

By deliberately adopting different hats during the decision-making process, leaders can ensure that they are considering all angles before making a final decision. This tool is particularly useful in team settings, where diverse perspectives can enhance the quality of the decision-making process.

The Six Thinking Hats model fosters creativity and encourages open-mindedness, making it a valuable tool for innovation, brainstorming, and problem-solving. However, it requires discipline and structure to ensure that participants stay focused on the task at hand and do not revert to their habitual thinking styles.

Appendix B: Real-World Case Studies of High-Stakes Scenarios

In the dynamic world of business, there are moments when leaders are faced with high-stakes scenarios—decisions that can determine the success or failure of an organization. Understanding how others have navigated such crises can provide valuable lessons. This appendix explores several real-world case studies of companies that faced significant challenges, detailing their responses and the results of their decisions. By examining these cases, we can extract key insights into strategic decision-making, crisis management, and long-term planning.

1. Apple's Comeback: Navigating Innovation and Market Relevance

In the mid-1990s, Apple was teetering on the brink of bankruptcy. The company had lost its innovative edge, and its products were seen as overpriced and niche. The leadership was in disarray, and Apple was losing market share to competitors like Microsoft and Dell. This was a high-stakes moment—Apple needed to either innovate or collapse.

Steve Jobs' return to Apple in 1997 marked a turning point. His leadership emphasized simplifying the product line, focusing on design, and ensuring seamless integration of hardware and software. The introduction of the iMac in 1998 was a bold decision. It featured a striking design that made computers appealing to the everyday user, departing from the traditional gray boxes of the time. This gamble paid off as the iMac became a massive success, reigniting interest in Apple products.

Apple's comeback is a prime example of a high-stakes scenario where decisive leadership and innovation were critical. Jobs streamlined the company's focus, placed a premium on user experience, and prioritized the creation of an ecosystem that locked consumers into the Apple brand. Today, Apple's continued success, with products like the iPhone and MacBook, demonstrates the long-term impact of those early decisions in a high-pressure environment. The key takeaway from this case is that businesses can recover from dire situations through bold innovation, strong leadership, and a clear strategic vision.

2. Toyota's Response to the 2010 Recall Crisis

In 2010, Toyota faced one of the largest and most publicized product recalls in automotive history. The company had to recall millions of vehicles due to reports of unintended acceleration caused by faulty floor mats and accelerator pedals. The crisis led to widespread media coverage, government investigations, and significant reputational damage. For a company that had built its brand on reliability and safety, this was a catastrophic scenario.

Toyota initially responded with denial and deflection, which only worsened the public perception of the company. However, after recognizing the gravity of the situation, Toyota's leadership shifted gears. They issued a public apology, halted production to focus on fixing the issue, and launched a massive communication campaign to regain customer trust.

Toyota also introduced a comprehensive quality control system that emphasized safety and reliability more than ever before. This long-term commitment to addressing the root causes of the recall was critical to the company's recovery. By focusing on transparency, taking responsibility, and implementing systemic changes, Toyota was able to rebuild its reputation.

The Toyota case illustrates the importance of acknowledging and addressing crises head-on. While the company initially fumbled its response, the eventual pivot to customer-centric solutions and long-term reforms was crucial. The lesson here is that, in high-stakes scenarios, a swift, honest, and decisive response is essential to mitigating damage and restoring trust.

3. Netflix vs. Blockbuster: Winning in a Disruptive Market

Netflix's rise and Blockbuster's fall is one of the most prominent examples of a company successfully navigating a high-stakes scenario while its competitor failed. In the early 2000s, Blockbuster was the dominant force in the movie rental industry. Meanwhile, Netflix, a fledgling company at the time, was pioneering a mail-order DVD rental model. Blockbuster had the opportunity to purchase Netflix for $50 million in 2000 but declined, considering it an insignificant player.

This decision marked a pivotal high-stakes moment. Blockbuster continued to focus on its traditional brick-and-mortar stores, while Netflix embraced technological disruption, shifting from mail-order DVDs to online streaming in 2007. By betting on digital transformation and consumer convenience, Netflix positioned itself as the future of home entertainment.

Blockbuster, on the other hand, was slow to adapt. By the time it tried to compete with Netflix's streaming model, it was too late. In 2010, Blockbuster declared bankruptcy, while Netflix's subscription base soared into the millions, establishing it as a dominant force in global media.

This case highlights the importance of recognizing shifts in consumer behavior and technological disruption. Netflix's ability to adapt, innovate, and take calculated risks, even when the stakes were high, allowed it to thrive in an industry undergoing massive changes. Blockbuster's failure to recognize these signals underscores the danger of complacency and the necessity for proactive decision-making in high-stakes environments.

4. BP and the Deepwater Horizon Disaster

In 2010, BP faced a catastrophic high-stakes scenario when the Deepwater Horizon oil rig exploded, leading to one of the worst environmental disasters in history. The explosion killed 11 workers and resulted in millions of barrels of oil spilling into the Gulf of Mexico. The disaster severely damaged BP's reputation, led to massive financial penalties, and resulted in significant regulatory changes for the oil and gas industry.

BP's initial response to the disaster was widely criticized. The company downplayed the scale of the spill, and its CEO at the time, Tony Hayward, made several public relations blunders, including famously stating, "I'd like my life back," which was viewed as insensitive. The company was also slow in its efforts to contain the spill, which only exacerbated the environmental and economic damage.

However, BP eventually committed to a long-term recovery strategy. It invested billions of dollars in cleanup efforts, compensated affected communities, and implemented stricter safety measures across its operations. BP's focus on repairing its damaged image and demonstrating corporate responsibility was essential to its survival, though the company still faces lingering reputational challenges.

The BP case demonstrates how poor crisis management in a high-stakes scenario can have lasting consequences. Swift, transparent, and empathetic communication, coupled with decisive action, is critical in mitigating damage. BP's eventual efforts to make amends were necessary, but the delayed response showed the perils of underestimating the severity of a crisis.

5. Johnson & Johnson's Response to the Tylenol Poisoning Crisis

One of the most famous examples of exemplary crisis management is Johnson & Johnson's response to the Tylenol poisoning crisis in 1982. Seven people in the Chicago area died after taking Tylenol capsules that had been laced with cyanide. This was a high-stakes situation for Johnson & Johnson—the company's flagship product was involved in a series of deaths, and public trust in the brand was at risk.

Despite the immediate financial cost, Johnson & Johnson acted decisively. The company ordered a nationwide recall of 31 million bottles of Tylenol, costing more than $100 million. It also worked closely with the FDA and other authorities to identify the source of the tampering and began developing tamper-proof packaging to prevent similar incidents in the future. The company's swift, transparent response, along with its focus on customer safety, helped restore public confidence.

Within a year, Tylenol had regained its market share, and Johnson & Johnson's reputation for putting consumer safety first was solidified. This case underscores the importance of prioritizing customer safety and acting swiftly in high-stakes situations. Johnson & Johnson's response is still considered a gold standard in crisis management.

Appendix C: Checklist for Crisis Management and Resolution

In high-stakes business scenarios, having a clear, actionable plan is essential for managing and resolving crises. When a crisis strikes, whether it's a product recall, a PR disaster, or a financial setback, a well-structured approach can mean the difference between recovery and long-term damage. This checklist is designed to provide leaders with a step-by-step framework for navigating crises with confidence and effectiveness.

1. Immediate Response

- Activate the Crisis Management Team: Assemble a dedicated team that includes senior leadership, legal advisors, PR professionals, and relevant department heads. This team should be responsible for decision-making and communications during the crisis.

- Assess the Situation: Quickly gather all available information about the crisis. Determine the scope of the issue, its impact on stakeholders, and the potential risks. It's critical to understand the severity of the situation before making any public statements.

- Establish Command and Control: Ensure that there is a clear chain of command, and designate a spokesperson to handle communications. This helps prevent confusion and ensures that the organization speaks with one voice.

- Contain the Damage: Take immediate action to stop the crisis from worsening. For example, in the case of a product defect, issue a recall. If there's a PR issue, release an initial statement acknowledging the problem while investigations are underway.

2. Communication Strategy

- Be Transparent and Honest: When a crisis occurs, trust is often the first casualty. To maintain or rebuild trust, it's essential to be transparent about what's happening. Avoid minimizing or deflecting the issue. Acknowledge the problem, express empathy for those affected, and communicate the steps being taken to resolve the situation.

- Keep Stakeholders Informed: Develop a communication plan for key stakeholders—employees, customers, investors, and the media. Regular updates should be provided as new information becomes available. Make sure that internal communications are just as thorough as external ones; employees should not hear news about the crisis from outside sources.

- Prepare for Media Inquiries: The media will likely play a significant role in shaping public perception of the crisis. Prepare your spokesperson with clear, concise messaging and anticipate potential questions. Avoid speculation, and stick to the facts.

- Use Social Media Wisely: Social media can be a

powerful tool for disseminating information quickly. However, it can also exacerbate a crisis if not used carefully. Ensure that your social media messaging is aligned with your broader communication strategy, and monitor online discussions for misinformation.

3. Problem Resolution

- Investigate the Root Cause: Conduct a thorough investigation to determine the root cause of the crisis. Whether it's a technical failure, a human error, or a larger systemic issue, understanding what went wrong is essential for preventing similar crises in the future.

- Implement Corrective Measures: Once the root cause is identified, take steps to address it. This may involve changing processes, updating technology, or implementing new training programs. The goal is to ensure that the issue is fully resolved and won't recur.

- Compensate Affected Parties: If customers, employees, or other stakeholders were harmed or inconvenienced by the crisis, consider offering compensation. This can range from refunds or replacement products to public apologies and community outreach initiatives.

4. Post-Crisis Evaluation and Learning

- Review the Crisis Response: After the immediate crisis has passed, conduct a comprehensive review of how the situation was handled. What went well? What could have been improved? This evaluation should involve all members of the crisis management team and key stakeholders.

- Document Lessons Learned: Crises can provide valuable learning opportunities. Document what was learned from the experience and incorporate these lessons into future crisis management planning.

- Update Crisis Management Plans: Based on the evaluation, update the organization's crisis management plans and protocols. Ensure that any gaps identified during the crisis are addressed, and make necessary changes to improve the organization's readiness for future crises.

5. Rebuild and Move Forward

- Rebuild Trust: Depending on the severity of the crisis, it may take time to rebuild trust with stakeholders. This will require ongoing communication, demonstrating that the organization has learned from the crisis, and consistently delivering on promises to improve.

- Monitor Long-Term Impacts: Crises can have long-term impacts on brand reputation, financial performance, and customer loyalty. Monitor these areas closely in the months following the crisis and take proactive steps to mitigate any lingering effects.

- Celebrate Recovery: Once the crisis has been resolved, take a moment to recognize the efforts of the crisis management team and the organization as a whole. This helps boost morale and reinforces the organization's resilience in the face of adversity.

Aspect	Company/Example	Key Actions	Outcome	Lessons Learned
Apple Comeback (1997)	Apple Inc.	Streamlined product line, focused on design & user experience	Became a market leader in innovation and profitability	Bold innovation, strong leadership, strategic vision can reverse dire situations.
Toyota Recall Crisis (2010)	Toyota	Issued public apology, halted production, improved quality control	Rebuilt customer trust, recovered brand reputation	Swift, honest response and long-term systemic change are key to crisis recovery.
Netflix vs. Blockbuster (2000s)	Netflix vs. Blockbuster	Shifted to digital streaming; adapted to consumer trends	Netflix dominates entertainment; Blockbuster went bankrupt	Recognizing disruption & adapting early are critical to long-term survival.
BP Deepwater Horizon (2010)	BP	Initially downplayed issue; later invested in cleanup & reforms	Suffered lasting reputational damage but avoided collapse	Early denial worsens crises; transparency and responsibility are crucial.
Tylenol Poisoning Crisis (1982)	Johnson & Johnson	Nationwide recall, developed tamper-proof packaging	Regained market share and public trust quickly	Prioritizing customer safety and swift, transparent action builds long-term trust.

Crisis Management Checklist	General business application	Assemble crisis team, communicate transparently, resolve root cause	Minimizes damage, restores operations, and rebuilds trust after a crisis	Proactive planning, clear communication, and learning from the crisis are key to effective resolution.

END

www.ingramcontent.com/pod-product-compliance
Lightning Source LLC
Chambersburg PA
CBHW070356230526
45471CB00006B/2602